W&R Jacob

Celebrating 150 Years of Irish Biscuit Making

Fr. Coffey: (Yawns, then chants with a hoarse croak) Namine.
Jacobs Vobiscuits. Amen.

Circe. *Ulysses*. James Joyce.

W&R Jacob

CELEBRATING 150 YEARS OF IRISH BISCUIT MAKING

Séamas Ó Maitiú

The Woodfield Press

This book was typeset by
Red Barn Publishing, Skeagh, Co. Cork for
THE WOODFIELD PRESS
17 Jamestown Square, Dublin 8
www.woodfield-press.com
e-mail: terri.mcdonnell@ireland.com

Publishing Editor
Helen Harnett

House Editor
Amy Hayes

A catalogue record for this title
is available from the British Library.

ISBN 0-9534293-1-8

Printed in Ireland
by Wood Printcraft

Contents

Chronology   vi

Picture Credits   vii

Acknowledgements   viii

Preface   ix

Brothers and Friends   1

Fire, Revolution – and Cream Crackers!   24

The Figs in the Fig Rolls   49

From Family Firm to National Stage   77

On the Move – A New Home in Tallaght   95

Jacob's in Literature   110

Partners/Directors of W. & R. Jacob Co., Dublin   112

Short Bibliography   115

Index   117

Chronology

1674/5   Richard Jacob flees to Ireland from England to escape religious persecution

1850   William and Robert Jacob place a notice in the *Waterford Mail* announcing their entry into the fancy biscuit market

1851   The production of biscuits on an industrial scale in Waterford

1852   The lease by William and Robert Jacob of premises in Peter's Row, Dublin

1853   Production under way in Peter's Row

1862   Death by drowning of Robert Jacob at Tramore

1863   William Frederick Bewley becomes a partner

1880   Fire destroys much of the Bishop Street premises

1885   The launch of the Cream Cracker

1897   The launch of mallow biscuits

1900   Coke replaced by coal to a large extent in ovens; Visit of Queen Victoria - shortly afterwards 'Royal Appointment' received by Jacob's

1902   Death of William Beale Jacob

1909   Visit of Lord Aberdeen to the factory, after which he addresses the workers in the Recreation Hall; football field at Rutland Avenue, Crumlin leased and subsequently bought

1912   Establishment of Jacob's factory at Aintree, Liverpool

1913   Great Dublin Lockout; hard line taken by George N. Jacob

1916   Jacob's taken over by rebels under Thomas McDonagh

1921   Free State troops briefly take over factory to prevent occupation by Republicans

1922   Creation of two separate companies in Dublin and Liverpool

1942   Death of George N. Jacob

1948   Loss of the export market by Dublin to Liverpool; Molyneux Church converted into Jacob's recreation hall

1957   Arrival of Boland's Biscuits in the marketplace

1961   Production of chocolate confectionery comes to an end

1963   Frankie Byrne's 'Women's Page' programme, sponsored by Jacob's, begins on Radió Éireann

1966   Jacob's and Boland's biscuit interests merge as Irish Biscuits; W. and R. Jacob become holding company

1968   Decision taken to move to Tallaght

1971	Extreme financial difficulties experienced by the company
1972	Boland's Deansgrange factory ceases production
1975	Tallaght plant officially opened by Justin Keating, Minister for Industry and Commerce
1977	Last biscuit baked at Bishop Street
1979	Associated Biscuit Manufacturers increase holding in Jacob's to 29.96%
1982	Nabisco buy out Associated Biscuit Manufacturers, and with it 29.6% of Jacob's
1990	In 1990, BSN Danone, buy the European operations of Nabisco including its share in Jacob's
1991	Jacob's of Dublin taken over by Groupe Danone

Acknowledgements

I have incurred many debts in the compilation of this history. In tracing Quaker connections, Joan Johnson of Waterford and Bill Wigham were most generous in answering my queries and supplying photographs. Rob Goodbody conducted me on a visit to the beautiful Quaker burial ground at Temple Hill, Blackrock, Co. Dublin to identify the Jacob family graves.

Frances Gilsenan, my first contact in Jacob's, made me, as an outsider, feel most welcome and introduced me to both current employees and pensioners who contributed to this story. I would like to thank her for her continued encouragement and support of the project. Jonathan Bewley, the last in a long line of that family associated with Jacob's stretching back to 1863, was most enthusiastic about the idea of a history and pointed out sources in Tallaght to me which might have remained hidden without his intervention. Denis Donoghue, company secretary at the time of writing, made available to me annual reports which proved most valuable. Meeting Gordon Lambert was most fruitful. His unrivalled knowledge of Jacob's was generously put at my disposal, my only regret being that I had only the space here to utilise a small fraction of it. Ex-employees of Jacob's were most generous with their memories of their work there, including Dan Dent, Billy McDonagh and Neville Wiltshire.

The kind guidance of Douglas Appleyard steered me clear of many pitfalls. His reading of the manuscript was close and expert and greatly improved my knowledge of the internal working of the company. Thanks to Amy Hayes and Orla Fee for proof-reading the manuscript, Brendan Lyons for typesetting and Mark Loughlin for designing the cover. Two ladies deserve special mention: the gentle nudging of Sharon Nolan of the Marketing Department in Jacob's to fulfill deadlines was most welcome, especially as the time from research to writing was so short. The encouragement, support and expert attention of Terri McDonnell of The Woodfield Press was, as usual, unfailing, and her enthusiasm for the book greatly lightened the workload.

Séamas Ó Maitiú

Preface

Generations of Irish people left school with the impression that Ireland had, in essence, little or no industrial history. Thankfully that view is changing. In the light of the new awareness of Ireland's admittedly small but not unimportant industrial past, it would have been remiss to let the years 2001 and 2002 slip by without marking in some way the birth, growth and indeed survival of a remarkable Irish enterprise. 2001 sees the one hundred and fiftieth anniversary of the production of biscuits by two Waterford brothers, William and Robert Jacob – the 'W. & R. Jacob' engraved on the irresistable biscuits that have been found on Irish and British tea-tables for generations. The year 2002 marks the centenary of William Jacob's death.

Having been brought up close to the heartland of the Jacob workforce in Bishop Street in Dublin, the most obvious, and to a child, the most important evidence of Jacob's presence was the weekly ration of broken biscuits brought home by an older cousin, a 'Jacob's girl'. However, of much more importance was the Jacob's weekly wage-packet, which supported many a south-side Dublin family, or, at least in the case of the thousands of young women, made a significant contribution to the meagre family budget.

Having begun my researches, the more I delved into the history of the company and spoke to the extended Jacob's community, the more I realised that all that could be accommodated in the time and space allotted to the present publication would be an outline of Jacob's history, and a flavour of how the great industry worked and was organised. There are literally thousands of Jacob's stories out there; unfortunately it was possible only to include a small selection of them here. There is ample scope for an extensive oral history project based on the experiences of Jacob's workers. Hopefully such a project will be undertaken.

The creativity and ingenuity, whether in relation to baking, engineering or marketing, that has gone into the enterprise over the century and a half has been colossal. This book is the first history of the company, and its aim is to provide for the general reader with an interest in Irish industrial and social history, whether connected with Jacob's or not, an outline of the founding, development and achievements of the firm – as the title states, to celebrate a great Irish institution. Go maire sé céad caoga bliain eile!

CHAPTER ONE

Brothers and Friends

In the year 1851, a young man, on his way home to Waterford from a business trip in England, noticed a well-situated spacious premises for sale which might suit the great plans he had in mind. The twenty-six year old William Beale Jacob had gone to England to investigate the latest methods employed in the manufacture of fancy biscuits, which were taking off in a big way at that time. He and his younger brother, Robert, were already making biscuits in their native Waterford and were particularly interested in finding out more about the application of steam machinery to the process, as they could barely keep up with demand from their two small premises.

The England that William visited was in a state of high excitement. The pride of British industry, its products and machinery, were on display in the Great Exhibition in the Crystal Palace in London. It is likely that William took the opportunity to pay the exhibition, which was attracting phenomenal crowds, a visit. The mood of optimism matched very well the feelings of William, on the point of making a great leap forward in the new industry of fancy biscuit-making. Indeed, so confident was William in the future of this new food product that, according to his son, he was considering completely selling up in Waterford and starting a new bakery in England, when the Dublin premises caught his eye.

The property that William noticed was a large vacant coach yard at numbers 5 and 6 Peter's Row, on the outskirts of Dublin's ancient industrial district known as the Liberties. The availability of such a suitable premises and the favourable terms on which he obtained them, clinched the matter for the young Mr Jacob – he would launch his enterprise in Dublin. William did not hesitate, and was shortly the possessor of the premises. So began the story of a great Irish food enterprise going strong to this very day.

QUAKER BACKGROUND

Of great relevance to our story is the fact that William Jacob and his brother, Robert, were members of the Religious Society of Friends, or Quakers. The Society of Friends was founded at the time of the English revolution in the seventeenth century by George Fox (1624–1691). Of the many sects that arose from the religious cauldron of revolutionary England, the Quakers survived and prospered. Their use of 'thee' and 'thou' and their practice of keeping hats on indoors originated with Fox's determination not to make signs of obeisance to any man, including the king. For Quakers, the spiritual life was understood in entirely personal terms so that they did not employ sacraments or other outward forms of worship. The doctrine of the Inward Light saw Quakers' speech as the prompting of the Spirit, and this developed into the style of silent worship of popular imagination. As any member may be 'moved by the Spirit' to witness, all members at a meeting for worship were potential ministers, including women. Quaker belief did not allow marriage to those outside the fold, and encouraged business partnerships only with fellow-Quakers. The positive benefits of the resultant close-knit community, however, had to be balanced by the negative consequences of this. Those who did marry non-Quakers suffered automatic 'disownment'. The same fate befell those who became bankrupt, a predicament seen as dishonest, as the money of others was put at risk. A paper of disownment signed by a member of the Jacob family survives. In 1824, one Henry Howis 'who was educated in the Profession of the Trust as held by us the people called Quakers disregarding the dictates thereof in his own mind, hath so far deviated as to run into many improper and unjustifiable practices'. Included in these practices was 'raising money on fictitious credit for long continuance'.

To minimise such a risk, Quakers kept a close eye on each other's commercial affairs. They trusted and helped each other, and took the sons of relations and fellow-Quakers as apprentices. This proved very successful for the conduct of business. This system, their honest dealings and plain living enabled them to grow prosperous as manufacturers, tradesmen, bankers, and merchants. They eventually came to dominate key eighteenth-century industries in Britain and Ireland. Quaker families became household names in the fields of iron-making, chemicals, pharmaceuticals and banking. In the nineteenth century they went on to play a key role in new industries such as shoemaking, biscuits and chocolate. Barclays, Lloyds, Price Waterhouse, Swan Hunter, Clarks' shoes, Wedgewood, Huntley and Palmer, Cadbury, Frys and Rowntree all have Quaker origins in England. In Ireland, famous Quaker business families include the Pims, Grubbs, Malcolmsons, Bewleys and, of course, the Jacobs. This is a remarkable achievement when one considers that the Friends, as the Quakers were also known, remained a tiny sect. They never numbered more than one per cent of the population in England or Ireland.

Quakers were known for their charity and humanitarianism. They espoused causes such as the abolition of slavery and prison reform and their charity during the Great Famine in Ireland is remembered to this day. Such was the milieu into which William and Robert Jacob were born.

THE JACOB FAMILY

The surname Jacob is a form of the Welsh Iago, and is also found in Cornwall in the form of Jago. In England the Jacob family were associated with certain well-defined areas in Somerset, Devon and Dorset. Among the followers of George Fox, the founder of the Quakers, was one Richard Jacob, a direct ancestor of William and Robert. The Quakers' forthright rejection of the rituals of the established church led to ostracisation and persecution. Such treatment led many of them to consider deserting England for new pastures where they might practise their religion free from the oppressive atmosphere of their homeland. Many fled to America, and some made their way to Ireland.

The Richard Jacob of our story, the son of another Richard Jacob and Alice Holcombe, was of the Devonshire branch of the family and was baptised in 1642. However, in his youth he became a fervent convert to Quakerism. This led to persecution and arrest by the authorities and he decided to move to Ireland. The exodus of the Jacob family to Ireland had an almost biblical air about it. In the year 1674 or 1675, Richard, his wife Joan and their six children, the eldest eleven years, travelled by horseback to Minehead in Somerset, and from that port set sail for Ireland. Richard, having so many mouths to feed, and displaying the industry so characteristic of Quakers, lost no time in setting himself up as a cutler in Cork, where three more sons were born.

Richard Jacob was the patriarch from whom a large and many-branched family would descend over the generations. His second son, also called Richard, resided in Limerick, and lived there until his death in 1725. This second Richard's only son, Isaac, was born in Limerick in 1703. At the age of nineteen he moved to Waterford and took over the business of his uncle, Joseph Jacob, who died in 1724. Letters of Isaac survived for many years in the Jacob family and they demonstrated that the characteristics of the later Jacob family were deep-rooted. While spiritual matters are to the fore, a keen interest in business matters is in evidence. A stern regard for accuracy and straight-dealing in all worldly affairs demonstrates Isaac's immersion in the virtues of the Quaker community. He became a well-known figure in Waterford, acting as clerk to the city's thriving Quaker meeting. He possessed a strong character with a taste for literature, and when he died in 1761, of what was called a 'nervous fever', he was widely mourned.

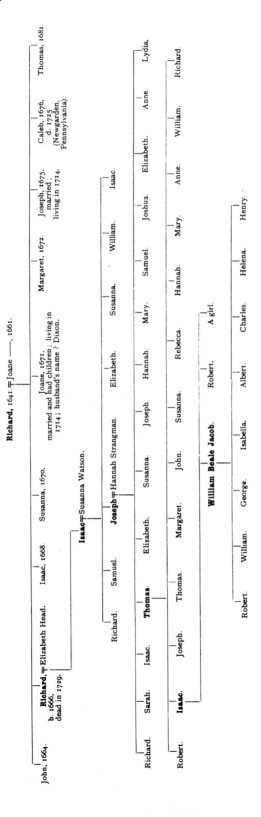

Family tree of Jacob family in Ireland (from Henry W. Jacob, *A History of the Families of Jacob of Bridgewater, Tiverton and Southern Ireland*, private circulation, Taunton, 1929).

His third son, Joseph, married Hannah Strangman of Mountmellick, and with money left him by his father, and with the good offices of his in-laws, became a partner in the firm of Jacob, Watson and Strangman, brokers and shipping agents. Waterford is a city with a rich maritime history, and in the eighteenth century, a substantial sea-trade was conducted from there. As well as ports in the south of England such as Bristol, Waterford ship-owners had a valuable trade with the rich fisheries of Newfoundland. Quakers were deeply involved in the maritime trade, especially the export of yarn from the Waterford hinterland to Minehead, whence Richard Jacob had begun his exodus a century before. At the high point of his prosperity and success, Joseph Jacob and his wife lived in King's Street, where the Waterford Meeting House also stood. In 1777 Joseph had a tablet affixed to their house bearing his initials and that of his wife together with the date, which could still be read some years ago.

However, within a few years of that date, Joseph was dead and the firm of Jacob, Watson and Strangman ruined. It had large interests on the island of St. Eustasia (now known as St. Eustatius) in the Dutch Caribbean, which at this period acted as a kind of exchange for goods passing between the old and new worlds. When the British defeated the Dutch at sea and seized the colony in 1780, everything on the island was confiscated despite a royal letter guaranteeing the safety of all goods and property of those engaged in legitimate trade. Most galling of all was an auction at which merchant's goods were sold at one-third their price – with previous owners not allowed to bid.

This was a particularly devastating blow to Joseph Jacob as he had a family of fourteen children. They were left destitute and scattered throughout the country. However, his third son, Thomas Strangman Jacob, overcame this knock to his early prospects and established a flourishing corn business. Born at Waterford in 1762, Thomas married Hannah Fennell Lecky of the family of the Irish historian, W. E. H. Lecky. Keenly aware of the pain caused by want, Thomas dug deep to help the needy in his native city. Two charities grateful to him for his bounty were the Waterford House of Industry and Waterford Fever Hospital. The precarious nature of business life at that time is demonstrated by the fact that Thomas Jacob also fell on hard times. The second son of Thomas and Hannah Jacob, Isaac, brings us to the involvement of the family in baking.

'TWICE BAKED BREAD'

The Oxford English Dictionary states that the word biscuit comes from the Latin 'biscotum (panem)', that is 'twice baked bread' and a version of

Joseph Jacob's House 18th Century

(Above) Joseph Jacob's house (centre), Waterford – despite having two doors, the house originally was all one.

(Below) Stone bearing the initials of Joseph Jacob and his wife Hannah (Strangman), great-grandparents of William Beale Jacob, and the date 1777, set in his house in Waterford. Joseph was to lose everything he had in 1780, when his property on the island of St. Eustasia was confiscated.

the word is found in all the Romance languages. Early biscuit-making arose from the need to provision ships going on long sea voyages with a baked food that would last the lengthy periods between ports. The two properties of the early nautical biscuit were that it was hard and dry. Shakespeare uses the simile 'as dry as the remainder bisket after a voyage'. So despised was the nautical biscuit after a long voyage that mariners would ceremoniously toss those remaining overboard on sight of their home port, and 'a biscuit toss' was a common sea-farers' expression.

In the early nineteenth century, the largest biscuit manufacturers were those supplying the navy. Ships' biscuits were often made by the navy itself in the victualling yards before ships set sail. The dough was mixed by hand and baked four times before being cut into rounds and placed in wooden casks or canvas bags and put on board ship. Another tradition of biscuit-baking also existed; this was the making of sweet or fancy biscuits by small bakeries. These were confections of fine flour and sugar mixed with fruit and juices. Housewives also made these at home. It was stated in 1865 that biscuit bakers held a middle path between pastry cooks and confectioners. In Germany and Austria the term 'zwieback' or 'twice-baked' was said to comprise a vast variety of small biscuit-like cakes.

Quakers were attracted to baking as it provided a basic, wholesome food – the very staff of life. Bread-baking, however, was hedged around by all sorts of rules and regulations, and profits from it were unspectacular. It was also wasteful as it had to be baked at night and the ovens could be idle during the day. The Quaker commitment to simplicity also turned them away from 'superfluities' with a preference for the food and (usually soft) drink industries. Contemplation of the famous Quaker tapestry, constructed by people from all over the world, based on an inspiration of Quakers in 1981, conveys this idea in a very direct way. From 'innocent trades', rural cottage industries such as weaving, pottery-making, shoe-making and baking, grew some of the greatest of British industries. Quaker-owned bakeries which began biscuit-making on an industrial scale included Huntley and Palmer, Carr and Peak, Freen.

The major biscuit manufacturers all began as small town bakers. The largest, Huntley & Palmer, began in 1822 in Reading. Joseph Huntley took advantage of the bustling business at the Crown Inn, a regular coach stop across the street from his bakery, by sending boys over with trays of biscuits for the travellers to purchase. J. D. Carr began making fancy biscuits in Carlisle in 1837. Demand grew. With the spread of the railways and the growth of tea-drinking, biscuits became the ideal snack. The new sweet food item had an aura of luxury about it, far removed from its despised nautical ancestor. Biscuits were refined and attractive to the nose and the eye, and became popular among middle-class women in particular who indulged in afternoon tea to break up the long monotonous afternoons at home. Biscuits did retain however one important trait inherited from the maritime variety – they kept well. Although a foodstuff, they were not as perishable as many others. Packed in an airtight tin they could last for weeks, even months.

To satisfy the increasing demand, Carrs of Carlisle investigated a steam biscuit-making machine they had heard of and installed one in 1838, the first concern in Britain to do so. The machine could make a ton of flour into biscuits in an hour.

JACOB'S BAKERY
This is the burgeoning business that Isaac Jacob became involved in, although he made only sea-biscuits. As his father had been in the corn trade, it is not surprising that the son became a baker. He sold bread and soon began to bake biscuits. The need to victual ships engaged in the thriving Waterford maritime trade provided an opportunity for an enterprising baker. An indication of the market in sea-biscuits can be gained from the fact that the Jacob family were not alone in that business. The Waterford directory of 1839 records that 'ship bread' was also being baked by Patrick Keiley of 9 George's Street.

The financial difficulties experienced by his father and grandfather impressed upon Isaac the extra need to be careful and prudent in his business dealings. In the spring of 1824 Isaac married Anne Beale, daughter of William Beale of Anngrove, near Mountmellick, of a family well-established in the woollen trade.

There was a strong Quaker presence in many Irish inland towns as well as in sea-ports such as Waterford and Cork. Indeed the Jacobs themselves had many such connections. Having so many children, the family had many branches. In Waterford, some of them became involved in importing iron and iron-founding from 1798. Involvement in the iron industry led a branch of the family to manufacture steam engines with the well-known Quaker family of Grubb in Clonmel in the 1830s and in the introduction of the first gas supply in Ireland in that town.

Isaac and Anne Jacob had three children. A son born at 33 Bridge Street in 1825 was named William Beale in memory of his mother's father. The second was a little girl who only lived a few hours, and a boy, Robert, was born in 1831. Isaac and his wife lived the whole fourteen years of their married life at 33 Bridge Street, except for the summer months when they could afford to retire to the countryside or the seaside. William states that his father was a reserved man, a devout Quaker, who became an elder in the Society of Friends in his native city. After an illness of several months, Isaac died on 23 March 1839 aged fifty.

William, only fourteen at the time, later described the day of his father's funeral and the effect that it had upon him:

> Upon one sad, gloomy day in that dreary spring I followed the remains of my father along the Quay of Waterford to his last resting place in a forlorn cemetery of the Friends off Manor Street, where he lies without a stone to tell who rests below, such memorials being strictly prohibited by the Society at that time. The dismal enclosure, overrun with weeds and relieved by not one solitary shrub or tree of any kind, was eminently calculated to impress my youthful imagination mournfully.

In the family annals, compiled by William, he describes his brother Robert's youth but modestly fails to devote space, unfortunately, to his own. Robert was born in the town of Mountrath on 14 June 1831 and was named after an uncle. This uncle, Isaac Jacob's brother, was an antiquarian who engaged in much family history research, which he handed on to William when he died at the early age of thirty-nine in 1828.

William speaks highly of his brother, an esteem heightened by subsequent tragedy. He describes him as intelligent and good-looking, with a fondness for books. He was educated in Waterford at a school conducted by a stern task-master, the Reverend Mr Price, and subsequently went to a Friends' school in Reading, run by a Mr Squire.

Birth certificate of Robert Jacob.

WATERFORD
GENERAL BAKERY.

WE beg respectfully to inform our numerous Customers and the Public of Waterford, that we intend opening next week the Premises,

No. 69, QUAY,

FOR THE SALE OF THE VARIOUS ARTICLES OF THE,

GENERAL AND FANCY BAKING TRADE,

In Connexion with our Establishment in Bridge-street.

The quality of our Bread is sufficiently known in Waterford to require from us no remark, further than to assure our Customers that no pains shall be spared on our part to continue to give a first-rate article at a moderate price.

HAVING COMMENCED THE MANUFACTURE OF THE

FANCY BISCUITS

Now in general use, we hope by attention to quality to secure for our

Waterford Made Biscuits

A portion of the present demand for those Imported from Carlisle and Edinburgh.

For the convenience of those who prefer Baking their own Bread we shall have a supply of Superfine Flour manufactured from the best Foreign and Irish Wheat.

We have also considerably reduced the Price of BARM, the retail rate of which will in future be

ONE HALFPENNY PER PINT
ONE PENNY PER QUART.
FOUR PENCE PER GALLON.

W. & R. JACOB.

Bridge-street, November 6th, 1850.

Advertisement placed by W. & R. Jacob in the *Waterford Mail*, 9 November, 1850.

Shop on right on the site of the original Jacob's bakery in Bridge Street, Waterford.

Artist's fanciful impression of Jacob's Waterford shop from the company's advertising.

WILLIAM AND ROBERT JACOB,

FANCY BISCUIT MANUFACTURERS,

WATERFORD.

Price List.

	Wholesale Price (Tins included) Per Doz. £ s. d.	Retail Price. Per Tin. s. d.	Retail Price. (Tins included) Per Tin. s. d	Allowed for Returned Tins. s. d.
RICH MIXED BISCUITS, consisting of Victoria, Champagne, Tunbridge, Coffee, Madeira, Lemon, Carraway, Wafers, Filberts &c.; an exquisite assortment in 5lb Tins	2 8 0	4 0	5 0	0 6
Do. Do. 3 lb.	1 10 0	2 6	3 0	0 4
Do. Do. 2 lb.	1 2 0	1 10	2 4	0 4
Do. Do. 1½lb.	0 15 0	1 3	1 6	0 3
Do. Do. 1 lb.	0 12 0	1 0	1 3	0 3
VICTORIA BISCUITS 14 lb.		12 6	..	1 3
Do. 2 lb.	1 4 0	2 0	2 4	0 4
Do. 1 lb.	0 13 0	1 1	1 4	0 3
CHAMPAGNE Do. 2 lb.	1 2 0	1 10	2 4	0 4
Do Do 1 lb.	0 12 0	1 0	1 3	0 3
PIC NIC Do. 14 lb.	..	7 0	..	1 3
VICTORIA GINGER Do. 14 lb.		11 6	..	1 3
MADEIRA Do. 2 lb.	1 2 0	1 10	2 4	0 4
Do. Do. 1 lb.	0 12 0	1 0	1 3	0 3
LEMON Do. 2 lb.	1 2 0	1 10	2 4	0 4
Do. Do. 1 lb.	0 12 0	1 0	1 3	0 3
TUNBRIDGE Do. 2 lb.	1 2 0	1 10	2 4	0 4
Do. Do. 1 lb.	0 12 0	1 0	1 3	0 3
GINGER Do. 2 lb.	1 2 0	1 10	2 4	0 6
Do. Do. 1 lb.	0 12 0	1 0	1 3	0 3
ORMSKIRK GINGER CAKES 5 lb.	2 6 0	3 10	4 8	0 6
Do. Do. 3 lb.	1 8 0	2 4	2 10	0 4
Do Do. 5 lb.	1 16 0	3 0	3 6	0 6
RICH GINGER CAKES 3 lb.	1 2 0	1 10	2 4	0 4
QUEEN'S BISCUITS 14 lb.		8 6	..	1 3
ARROWROOT Do. 14 lb.		8 3	..	1 3
ALBERT Do. 2 lb.	1 2 0	1 10	2 4	0 4
Do. Do. 1 lb.	0 12 0	1 0	1 3	0 3
CHOICE DESSERT CAKES, a rare assortment of delicacies peculiarly adapted for Dessert, and for the decoration of the Supper Table 1 lb.	0 18 0	1 6	2 0	0 3

If kept in Tins and in a dry place, these Biscuits will preserve their crispness and flavour for a long period.

				80 lbs.	50 lb.	30 lbs.
PIC NIC	BISCUITS, in Barrels, per Cwt.			46s.	47s.	48s.
FANCY	Do.	„	„	58s.	59s.	60s.
QUEEN'S	Do.	„	„	58s.	59s.	60s.
ARROWROOT	Do.	„	„	56s.	57s.	58s.
CABIN	Do.	„	„	27s.	28s.	29s.
LUNCH	Do.	„	„	30s.	31s.	32s.

PREPARED BISCUIT POWDER IN AIR-TIGHT TINFOIL PACKAGES---3s. 6d. PER DOZEN.

These Biscuits, Manufactured from the best materials, and by powerful Machinery, will be found equal to any yet offered to the trade.— Amongst the more expensive descriptions are some which may be justly considered to form the *ne plus ultra* of Biscuit Manufacture.

Carriage free to London, Dublin, Liverpool, Bristol, and all towns having direct communication by Steam Boat or Rail with Waterford

Waterford price list for Jacob's biscuits about October 1851: over a dozen varieties of biscuits were available and an assortment of cakes. Carriage was free to London, Dublin, Liverpool, Bristol and all towns having direct communication by steam boat or rail to Waterford. This was probably a limiting factor and precipitated a move to Dublin.

As a child, Robert was timid and bookish. But as he grew older, the outdoors gradually took a hold on him. He developed a passion for the countryside and delighted in climbing cliffs, exploring caves, swimming and boating. William described the change in his brother: 'To him who had been so timid when a boy, danger became a delight, and he once told me that if he observed a particularly dangerous spot on a cliff or height, it seemed as if he felt a positive longing to run the risk of reaching it as for the possession of some coveted luxury'.

The bakery in Bridge Street was in the hands of their mother, Anne, until such time as the brothers were of age to take it over. William hints that Robert was in charge of the book-keeping and became a commercial traveller for the business. Again he speaks with great regard of the abilities of his brother in these matters: 'My brother was placed in our office where he evinced industry and ability such as I am afraid I never did when I was graduating there'.

Robert married Hanna Maria Walpole of Waterford in 1856, and his wife's brother, James, became his companion in all his excursions. William had married Hannah Hill Newsom on 1 August 1850. The fact that he was beginning to establish a family encouraged William to take advantage of the growing business opportunities he saw in biscuits.

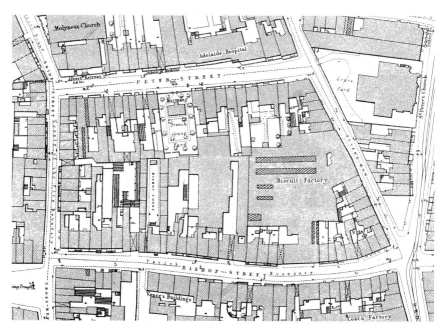

1892 map showing the extent of the factory a little more than a decade after the disastrous fire of 1880 (original scale of 1:1056 reduced).

Two months after his marriage, William, having consulted Robert, felt that the time was right to enter the fancy biscuit business in a big way. To facilitate this it was necessary to obtain a new premises. These were found at the Quay, the glory of Waterford. An advertisement appeared in the *Waterford Mail* on 9 November 1850 announcing that the Waterford General Bakery, already established at Bridge St., was opening a new premises at No. 69, The Quay. The brothers informed the public that as well as the usual general and fancy baked products, including their well-known bread, flour, both Irish and foreign, and barm, they had commenced manufacturing fancy biscuits, which were 'now in general use'. They appealed to the good people of the city to help them secure for their Waterford-made biscuits a portion of the demand for biscuits imported from Carlisle and Edinburgh. The new premises were well chosen. A description of the city found in the *New Commercial Directory for the Cities of Waterford and Kilkenny*, published in 1839, crowned its description of Waterford with a eulogy on the Quay:

> The city is beautifully situated on the southern bank of the Suir, about 16 miles from its influx into the sea. It extends principally along the margin of the river. . . The city is remarkably healthy and the air is pure. On the opposite side of the Suir are some lofty hills, from which the city is seen to great advantage, having in front the river and the splendid Quay, extending one mile in length, with scarcely any interruption from the Bridge to the mouth of John's River. In front of the Quay is a flagged footway, and a macadamised carriage road, and the path along the river is partly separated from these, and forms a beautiful promenade, the whole being lighted by a double row of gas lamps, which, with those in the various shops, gives to the whole a most brilliant and pleasing appearance.

The Jacobs lost no time in equipping their new premises. A pair of rollers for dough, each 14 inches long and four inches in diameter, was obtained to roll the dough into sheets having being first braked (kneaded). These rollers were made by a company called Slight. They also obtained two cutting machines, one for 'Pic-Nic' biscuits and one for 'Fancy' biscuits. The machines were hand-operated and worked, as the brothers themselves stated, 'on the stamping principal, with fifty or sixty cutters in each'.

As sales expanded, the brothers quickly needed more equipment. On the nineteenth of February 1851, they wrote to Messrs T. & T. Vicars of Liverpool, who described themselves as 'engineers, millwrights, machinists, and ironfounders – patentees of improved ovens and machinery for

Robert Jacob; his death by drowning at Tramore, Co. Waterford, in 1861 was a great blow to the fledgling firm.

bread and biscuit-making'. The Jacobs explained the background to their enquiry:

> We have received a circular of yours addressed to a party who resides with us, and we should feel obliged by your sending us some further particulars as to the Biscuit Machinery you have made. We have recently added that branch of trade to our other business, and have got some of our machinery from Edinburgh.

Having informed Vicars of the machinery they already had, they outlined their requirements. The enquiry showed a very practical turn of mind on the brothers' part, and is a forerunner of the innovative and inventive mind that the firm of Jacob's brought to their engineering problems up to the present day, in many cases actually inventing the machinery needed to solve the problem at hand themselves. They wrote:

William Beale Jacob.

We shall be obliged by your informing us whether you have a machine to which separate sets of cutters can be attached, so that after making a lot of one kind, you can take the plate out, put in another, and turn out a lot of different biscuits. If you have it send us the plans. We want a mixing machine, and a pair of fluted braking rollers such as could be worked by hand, as we have not steam power at present. If you think you could give us these, and such as you could engage to work well, please send us estimate and plans. . . We presume you have made some of Haylock's machinery, as well as for other large English Houses in this trade, such as Barrington of Dublin.

THE MOVE TO DUBLIN

The latter comment suggests that English biscuit-makers were, even at this early stage, moving to Dublin to take advantage of the market there. Barringtons were biscuit-makers of Eustace Street in the city. The Jacobs also enquired about what they called a 'railway oven'. This was an early form of conveyor belt-type of machinery, also known as a travelling oven, where the dough moved through a long oven and came out baked at the

William Beale Jacob and his wife, Hannah.

far end. Biscuit-making had reached a higher state of mechanisation than one might think.

As has been noted, family accounts of the move from Waterford state that the brothers seriously thought of establishing in England. The close network of Friends extended from England to Ireland, and indeed America. Added to this is the fact that Robert had received a Quaker education in England, and that it is likely that William did also. With these connections, the Jacob brothers would have had close relations with many prominent Quaker business families in England. So an opening there would have come to their attention. The move to Dublin appears to have been a second option, clinched by the fortuitous availability of a suitable premises. Certainly, a move from Waterford suggested itself very early after the establishment of the bakery on The Quay. The bright prospects in fancy biscuits became apparent to the Jacobs by the huge success that their efforts in Waterford were met with. Within a very short time a thriving business was built up, with customers in many parts of Ireland and England. If a move to England with its huge potential market was not undertaken, the brothers felt that a move to Dublin, the distribution centre of Ireland, was a necessity.

The Dublin coachmaking company from which the Jacobs obtained their premises was Thomas Palmer and Sons, which traded at Nos. 5 and 6 Peter's Row. The Dublin directories list Thomas Palmer at No. 3 Peter's Row from as far back as 1797. Thom's Directory of 1853 lists the 'steam biscuit factory' of William and Robert Jacob there.

An 1852 memorial of the transaction between Palmer and the Jacob brothers is found in the Registry of Deeds, Dublin. William and Robert obtained the property for £160, subject to clearing a mortgage of £500 held by Palmer. The premises consisted of a dwelling house, coach house, 'back grounds', and yard, stated to have formerly belonged to Anne Radcliff and previously by Edward Lysaght. The property was bound by the west side of Whitefriar Street, Peter's Row and 'Big Butter Lane' also known as Bishop Street. Palmer was stated to be of Leamore Park, Co. Wicklow, while the Jacobs were described as biscuit manufacturers of the City of Waterford.

A study of further records in the Registry of Deeds shows that other well-known Quaker families in Dublin were involved in the development of the Jacob business; in June 1861 property dealings between William and Robert Jacob and Samuel Bewley and Charles Bewley Pim are recorded, and in 1874 further dealings between the same parties are noted.

The new biscuit factory on the edge of the Liberties was ideally situated, having excellent transport links to the city and the surrounding countryside on one of the main arteries in and out of the city. The traditional weaving industry of the Liberties was in decline at this period, so the coming of any new industry was a boon to the area. The Liberties and its environs would provide an abundant supply of labour then and in the years to come.

While location undoubtedly played a part in the success of the Jacobs' enterprise, timing was even more crucial. The year 1851 saw a recovery in the post-famine Irish economy. Rising prosperity both in countryside and town left many farming and middle-class, and some working class families, with a little to spend on luxuries. In the food category, fancy biscuits fitted the bill perfectly. The habit of consuming such new food items was allied to the spread of tea-drinking in these islands, which in the latter half of the nineteenth century spread down the social scale – like so much other fashionable customs. Tea, the preserve of the wealthy in the eighteenth and early nineteenth centuries began to fall in price and come within the resources of the middle class and then the workers. Two developments helped this move. In 1833, the monopoly of the East India

Brussels-made medal presented to W. & R. Jacob at the Dublin Industrial Exhibition of 1865.

Huguenot graveyard off Peter Street in use as recreation area for Jacob's workers.

Company was broken and tea became more freely available. In the 1840s, the Quaker firm of Bewley began to import and blend their own tea in Ireland. Shortly after the ending of the monopoly, enterprising colonial growers began to experiment with the growing of tea in India. This proved a great success and it shortly began to rival China as the source of supply for Europe. All this combined to boost supply and push down prices.

It is said that the Jacobs took quite a number of skilled workers with them from Waterford to Peter's Row, giving us an indication that the

Waterford business was thriving. For the time being, Robert remained in Waterford to look after business there. Business ledgers from 1855 on show a remarkably widespread network of outlets for Jacobs' products. Much of this must have been established before the move to Dublin as it would have been remarkable to have built it up in such a short period of time. As we have seen, William paid tribute to the popularity of his brother among their early customers around the country. A ledger in the company archives for 1855 shows that Robert was an extremely busy commercial traveller. The firm was trading in nearly every county in Ireland and was exporting to England.

Important customers in Dublin were: Kinahan and Co.; William Valentine's shops in Brunswick Street and Britain Street; Samuel Bewley; The European Hotel; The Canton Tea Co.; James Weir; Patrick Dunn, Rathgar; Mrs. Hogg, Rathmines; and Thomas Daniel, Leinster House, also in Rathmines. A number of these establishments, Thomas Daniel's for instance, were the common Irish combination of grocery shop and public house.

In the ledger we find that the Waterford branch of the firm, also called W. & R. Jacob, was supplying unspecified goods to the Dublin branch. By the end of 1855, the Jacobs were trading with just under one thousand establishments in towns and cities such as Wexford, Kilkenny, Carrickfergus, Belfast and Tralee in Ireland and Bridgewater, Bristol, Bath, Falmouth, Plymouth, Redruth, St. Ives, St. Anstell and Liverpool in England. The fact that many of these places were ports suggests that either the sale of sea-biscuits was still important or that they were chosen because they were points of export or import from Ireland.

BUSINESS EXPANDS

Hard figures corroborate the great expansion of the business that this network of outlets suggests. In the first year of production in Dublin, the capital of the business was £861 and the sales for the year were valued at £4,653. By the end of 1859, sales had more than quadrupled to £21,124.

Jacob's were only a short while in production in their Dublin premises when an opportunity arose to display their wares to a wide audience and show that they had arrived on the Irish industrial scene. One of the great highlights of the Victorian age was the opening of the Great Exhibition at the Crystal Palace in London in 1851, probably visited by William. This started a craze for exhibitions which lasted for decades. William Dargan, the great Irish railway entrepreneur decided to hold an Irish industrial exhibition in Dublin in 1853. Visitors to the magnificent exhibition buildings on the lawn of Leinster House were no doubt highly impressed with the selection of fancy and plain biscuits on display by W & R Jacob of Peter's Row found in the miscellaneous manufacturers and small wares section.

While on the topic of exhibitions, Jacobs entered their produce in the Dublin International Exhibition of 1865 and won a medal for the excellent quality of their biscuits, one of thirteen awarded for United Kingdom produce. Competition included entries from Peek, Frean & Company, Dockhead, London, and from manufacturers in Cork and bakers by the name of Perry in Dublin. The fine medal won on that occasion is still in existence.

The range of equipment expanded to meet demand. A long-anticipated step forward was taken on 14 August 1852 when the Jacob brothers purchased a five horse-power steam engine from Vicars of Liverpool to add to the original Peter's Row equipment of a cutting machine and two hand-ovens. The engine was obtained 'not fixed or packed, but as stood at Liverpool', at the bargain price of £100. No doubt great excitement attended the arrival and installation of the engine at Peter's Row. Jacobs could now describe themselves as possessing a 'steam factory', a term of some glamour in the 1850s. A travelling or 'railway' oven was purchased at the same time for £120 and a pair of fourteen-inch rollers for £40. This new equipment was augmented in 1854 with the arrival of two more hand ovens, and, in 1857, two more travelling ovens. A notable piece of equipment arrived in Peter's Row from Vicars in April 1858. This was a cutter with the legend 'W & R Jacob' fixed in type. So began the engraving of the famous name on biscuits known to households in Ireland and Britain ever since.

As we have seen, Robert remained in Waterford to look after the business there, but by 1858 the Dublin factory was so successful, it was decided to sell the Waterford premises and for Robert to move to Dublin. The Waterford premises were sold, complete with six ovens and a bread room. *Thom's Directory* for 1858 lists two other premises besides Peter's Row under the names of William and Robert Jacob, namely a premises in Lower Camden Street and one in George's Street. While it is only speculation, it is likely that these two properties, both near the biscuit factory, were used by the brothers as residences.

TRAGEDY STRIKES
Business prospered. However, after ten years of hard work and continuous expansion, tragedy struck. In the summer of 1861, Robert undertook a continental tour with his brother-in-law, during which they ascended

the Ortler Spitz mountain in the Tyrol, 12,800 feet above sea-level. Their spirit of adventure got the better part of their discretion and they found themselves lost on the mountain as night fell. They spent a terrible night crouched upon a narrow ledge of rock overhanging a precipice, exposed to a severe thunderstorm and in a semi-frozen condition. However, luck was with them on this occasion and they descended the dangerous slippery slope the next morning none the worse for their experience.

The two companions returned home, their love for nature and the great outdoors in no way diminished by their Austrian ordeal. October of that year found Robert and James Walpole on an Autumn excursion to Tramore, a seaside resort in County Waterford. On Sunday 13 October they left their lodgings for a walk on the cliffs before dinner. They were never seen alive again. Robert's body was found nearby the next day and that of James many miles along the coast some days later. The day was windy and it is thought that they went to see the effects of the storm on a well-known coastal feature, the Puffing Hole, near the local landmark known as the Metal Man. Robert left a widow and two children, Ernest, born in 1859 and Edith in 1857.

A feature of the business life of Quakers was that when fresh blood usually provided by large Victorian families failed, the extended family, or friends, could be called on to create new partnerships to add fresh stimulus to the enterprise. This is the course that was followed by William Jacob after the tragic death of his younger brother. William felt that a new partner was needed to take Robert's place. As Quakers living in the Waterford area, the Jacob and Bewley families were close. In 1822, one Samuel Bewley was apprenticed to Joshua Jacob, ironmonger, of Waterford. The partner chosen to replace Robert in 1863 was William Frederick Bewley. However, it is interesting that, although he was only involved with the firm for less than ten years, Robert's name is commemorated to this day in the name W. and R. Jacob.

In 1864, trade commenced in North Wales, but on the home front temporary competition was felt from John Chaytor Grubb's biscuit factory in Dublin.

In 1878, having worked in the factory for six years, William's second son, George Newsom Jacob, also became a partner. By this time another family member, William's brother-in-law, George Joshua Newsom, had, in typical Quaker fashion, joined the partnership and remained involved in the business until his death in 1897. The extent to which the firm had grown by this stage is seen in the value of the shares listed in a partnerships deed drawn up between these parties in 1879:

William Beale Jacob	£11,733 15s. 3d.
William Frederick Bewley	£7,822 10s. 1d.
George Joshua Newsom	£6,707 6s. 7d.
George Newsom Jacob	£1,139 6s. 7d.
Total	£27,402 18s. 6d.

As business thrived, more factory space was needed. Bit by bit more adjacent property was acquired until Jacob's eventually took up the entire block bounded by Bishop Street, Peter's Row, Peter Street and Bride Street. Some very historical and interesting properties were subsumed by the factory. In Peter Street stood the chapel of the non-conformist Huguenots built in 1711 and commonly known as 'French Peter's' to distinguish it from the Church of Ireland parish church of St. Peter in nearby Aungier Street. Attached to the Huguenot chapel was a graveyard. The church was replaced by a mortuary chapel in 1825 and the last burial took place there in 1878. The Jacob's factory eventually enclosed the graveyard and it became known to Jacob's workers as the 'The Green' and was used for rest and recreation at break times. It was reported in the Dublin press in 1960 that a French girl, Marie Emanuelle De Blacquer, working in Jacob's, found an ancestor lying there. This link between a Quaker firm and the other great community of religious émigrés to Ireland, the Huguenots, is interesting. The Huguenots had a lasting impact on the economic development of Ireland, becoming deeply involved in banking and commerce. Among those buried in Peter Street were Gabriel Béranger, the landscape draughtsman, who recorded buildings and monuments in Ireland between 1760 and 1780 and Jean Du Bedat, who established the first sugar refinery in Ireland, and members of the Le Fanu family. The remains buried there were removed to Mount Jerome Cemetery, Harold's Cross in 1968. A special Act of the Oireachtas, the Huguenot Cemetery (Dublin) Act, 1965, was required to carry this out.

Around 1900, when the bakehouse was extended and a new power house built, the iron foundry of Tonge and Taggart, another famous Dublin firm, was taken over. Another notable building obtained by Jacob's was Molyneux House, on the corner of Bride Street and Peter Street. Built in 1711 by Thomas Molyneux, an army physician, the house was an impressive brick-fronted structure with many striking stone decorations. These included a Molyneux family coat of arms surmounting the front door. The house was bought by Philip Astley in the late 1770s. Astley was an equestrian entertainer and built a large amphitheatre at the back stretching to Bride Street where for many years equestrian and other

THE BISCUIT FACTORY, AINTREE

As limited space round the Dublin factory precluded extensions there, the building of the factory illustrated below was commenced in 1910. The 60 years' experience acquired in Dublin was drawn upon in planning the construction and equipment of this factory, which contains every known facility in the manufacture of biscuits of the highest quality. Situated practically in the open country, its position allows for the expansion which the ever increasing demand for Jacob & Co's biscuits constantly calls for. Railway sidings and private roads ensure uninterrupted supplies of ingredients and the rapid despatch of the finished article.

THE BISCUIT FACTORY, DUBLIN.

Established in 1851, on a very small scale, the factory has since grown enormously, and some idea of its size can be gained by studying the picture on this page. The floor space is approximately 14 acres, and an average of 3,000 operatives are in constant employment. The factory is fitted with the most modern machinery and equipment obtainable and is bright and airy throughout.

It is in the Dublin factory that biscuits are specially baked and packed for despatch Overseas and this important Export business is steadily increasing in volume so that there is hardly a Market in the World where Jacob & Co's biscuits are not known and appreciated.

W & R JACOB & CO LTD DUBLIN, IRELAND.

Artist's view of the Dublin and Liverpool factories.

A colourful selction of biscuits for the children's market.

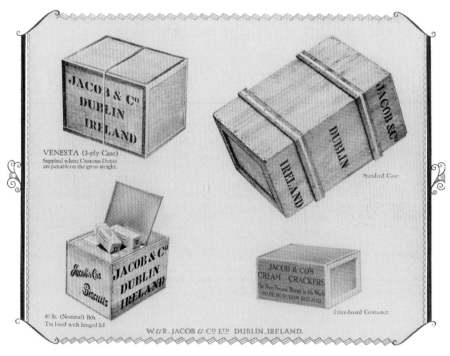

Packing in which biscuits were sent all over the world before World War II.

Tins displaying popular assortments.

Early packaging of the famous Jacob's Cream Crackers.

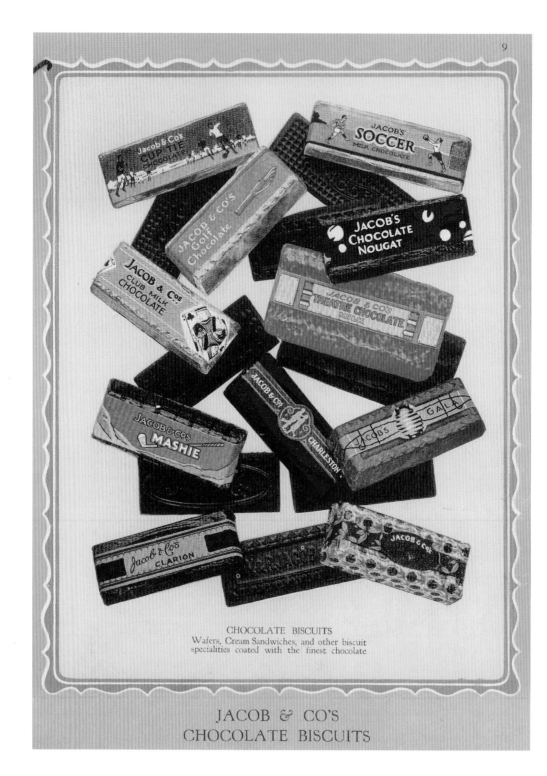

CHOCOLATE BISCUITS
Wafers, Cream Sandwiches, and other biscuit
specialities coated with the finest chocolate

JACOB & CO'S
CHOCOLATE BISCUITS

'Club' bars launched in 1901, extended to a wide variety.

performances took place. In 1815, the premises became the Molyneux Institute to care for the female blind. This moved to Leeson Street in 1862. The house was demolished by Jacob's in 1943 to make room for garages. The chapel of the Molyneux Institute, on Bride Street, was retained by Jacob's and served as the company Recreation Hall for many years.

Expansion took place also in these early days by way of mergers and take-overs. In 1874, a Cork Quaker firm trading as Baker and Co., steam biscuit-manufacturers, French Street, was taken over by Jacob's. Baker and Co. consisted of the partnership of Samuel Newsom, John Charles Newsom, Samuel Henry Newsom and George Baker. Jacob's bought their equipment on condition that they gave up manufacturing biscuits and would take their supply from Jacob's in future. Further conditions were imposed. Baker and Co. agreed not to sell any portion of the residue of their machinery or ovens to any person in Ireland without the consent of W. and R. Jacob and Co. and to use all necessary precautions to prevent any Irish house from purchasing the residue under the name of anyone residing outside of Ireland. Under these trade arrangements, Jacob's in effect took over the whole biscuit trade of the Cork firm.

Within three decades of that bold and imaginative step of William Jacob in obtaining the old coach yard at Peter's Row, Jacob's biscuit factory had become an institution in the industrial and commercial life of Dublin, and eventful years were to come.

CHAPTER TWO

Fire, Revolution – and Cream Crackers!

This chapter covers three eventful and disruptive episodes in the life of the factory, one pertaining only to Jacob's, and the others having a bearing on the life of the nation.

Disaster struck Jacob's in one fell swoop on the night of Thursday 30 January 1880. As huge temperatures are needed night and day in the factory, fire is always a danger and on that night a huge conflagration broke out in Jacob's factory. Work had discontinued as usual at 6 p.m. and everything appeared in order. It is not known at what time exactly the fire broke out, but it was noticed at nine-thirty. It appears to have broken out at the Bishop Street side of the premises and so could not be connected to the boiler house, a prime suspect in such outbreaks, which was at the other end. However, it quickly extended to the whole length of the factory, including the bakery, the boiler house and ultimately every part of the premises except offices along the frontage at Peter's Row.

The alarm was raised in the William Street fire brigade station shortly before ten o'clock, but apparently had already been noticed by the ever-vigilant Captain Ingram, head of the Dublin fire brigade. The brigade from William Street and Winetavern Street turned out as rapidly as possible, and by the time they arrived on the scene, the situation was very serious.

Captain Ingram had great difficulty obtaining access to the premises, but eventually the entrance at Peter's Row was burst open. The brigade had great difficulty in trying to fight the fire in the very confined space of Peter's Row. Even today the street is very narrow, but in 1880 it was lined on one side by tenement houses, inhabited by a large number of poor people. To make matters worse, these families and those in Bishop Street, another very narrow street, began to panic and pile up their furniture in the street prior to evacuation. This impeded the work of the fire brigade and became a fire hazard in itself. The fire was so intense by eleven o'clock that families in the other streets at a greater remove from the building also began to evacuate their premises.

The flames were jumping high into the sky with very little smoke, and by now could be seen from all parts of the city. A strong wind was blowing and sparks from the fire set the chimneys of a number of the surrounding tenements on fire, but the work of the firemen prevented any of them being consumed.

The Bishop Street factory at the time of the 1913 lockout.

The spectacle brought out a huge number of onlookers from all parts of the city, especially from the Coombe, which, according to the following day's newspaper report:

> would seem to have been emptied of its male population, at least by the large and rather disorderly crowds that blocked up all the approaches to the scene of the occurrence. These crowds at first were a serious impediment, and it was only by the expenditure of considerable force by bodies of police that they could be driven back and kept in check. In the end a party of the 77th Regiment, from Ship Street barracks, under the direction of Captain W. S. Wood, arrived, and completed the work of clearing the streets.

Five lines of hose were brought into play, one from Peter Street, one from Peter's Row and three from Bishop Street. The greatest difficulty was found in extinguishing the fire in the area of the factory where the butter and fatty matter were stored. The flames kept flaring up in that area, but were eventually brought under control between one and two o'clock.

The factory was substantially destroyed, apart from the buildings facing Peter's Row. An early newspaper report valued the damage at £30,000, and went on to claim that the premises and stock were almost entirely covered by insurance spread among a number of insurance

LIVERPOOL OFFICES & WAREHOUSES
286 to 304 Scotland Road.

LONDON OFFICES & WAREHOUSES
DOCKHEAD. S.E.

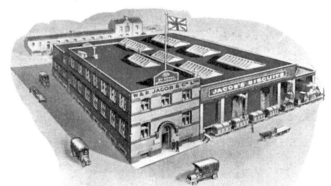

MANCHESTER WAREHOUSES :- Trafford Park.
SALE ROOM :- 21, Fennel St.

Jacob's English depots in 1911.

companies. Two men were slightly injured in the inferno. The steam engine with a temporary vertical boiler and some of the other machinery were in operation again after a short time. A store in Clarendon Street was rented and the packed tins of biscuits were sent there for labelling and dispatch. Carr's of Carlisle and two un-named Scottish firms manufactured a number of lines of biscuits for Jacob's for a period, mainly with cutters sent from Dublin.

REBUILDING

There was very little delay in rebuilding. The work was carried out by the well-known Dublin firm of W. F. Beckett, the father of the playwright. The rebuilding included the erection of a new packing loft; however three years afterwards another fire took place in the upper floor, and when rebuilding took place this time, an extra floor was added to the loft. This was the Mallow Department and stationery stores in later years. In 1889, Numbers 37, 38 and 39 Bishop Street were bought and a new building erected.

Continued building went on all through the 1890s. In 1892, the registered offices of Jacob's moved around the corner from 5, 6 and 7 Peter's Row to 28, 29, 30 and 31 Bishop Street, and the premises of the company was generally referred to as 'Bishop Street' from then on. In 1898 a new tank tower was erected. The following year old houses were bought and absorbed in an engineering shop and stores. In 1902, the factory's own power house in Peter Street was completed. In 1905, the factory was further extended to include from 39 to 44 Bishop Street.

After the fire, production was in full swing again before the end of 1881. The re-opening of the factory gave Jacob's an opportunity to advertise its products in the press. The appeal was very much in the 'Buy Irish' mould. The management supported 'the present most important movement in favour of promoting Irish industry', and went on to 'trust that those who have hitherto used IMPORTED biscuits and cakes will give the genuine Irish articles manufactured by W. and R. Jacob and Co. a fair trial, and thus assist in giving employment to Irish work people which all acknowledge to be so urgently needed'. Adverting to imports, the firm stated that 'the use of imported biscuits and other articles that can be made as well in Ireland is as injurious to the general prosperity of the country as it is generally unnecessary'.

This quick rebuilding and expansion is an indication of the buoyancy of the trade, all the more remarkable when it is set in the context of a recession in business in Dublin and in Ireland in general which lasted

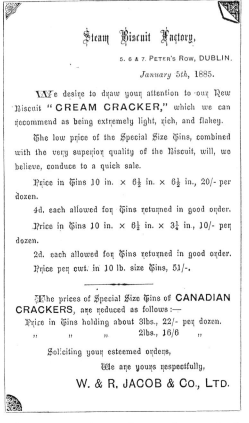

Steam Biscuit Factory,

5, 6 & 7, PETER'S ROW, DUBLIN.

January 5th, 1885.

We desire to draw your attention to our New Biscuit "CREAM CRACKER," which we can recommend as being extremely light, rich, and flakey.

The low price of the Special Size Tins, combined with the very superior quality of the Biscuit, will, we believe, conduce to a quick sale.

Price in Tins 10 in. × 6½ in. × 6½ in., 20/- per dozen.

4d. each allowed for Tins returned in good order.

Price in Tins 10 in. × 6½ in. × 3¼ in., 10/- per dozen.

2d. each allowed for Tins returned in good order.

Price per cwt. in 10 lb. size Tins, 51/-.

The prices of Special Size Tins of CANADIAN CRACKERS, are reduced as follows :—

Price in Tins holding about 3lbs., 22/- per dozen.

„   „   „   2lbs., 16/6   „

Soliciting your esteemed orders,

We are yours respectfully,

W. & R. JACOB & CO., LTD.

Leaflet printed in 1885 to announce the introduction of Cream Crackers.

throughout much of the 1870s and 1880s; for instance, the big Quaker cotton firm of Malcolmson of Portlaw, Co. Waterford collapsed in 1874. The slump led to the flooding of the Irish market with cheap imports from England, including biscuits.

In 1883, the four Jacob's partners decided that the time had come to form a limited company. Capital of £50,000 was raised by the selling of 500 shares at £100 each. The four partners became its first Board of Directors and W. F. Bewley and George N. Jacob, the third son of William, became its first Managing Directors. At the same time three other sons of William, Albert, Charles and William, entered the business.

LAUNCH OF THE 'CREAM CRACKER'

Hot on the heels of the formation of a limited company came Jacob's greatest success on the production side. Inventions and innovations are often surrounded by myth. Success due to careful research followed by a long period of trial and error are often ascribed in the popular imagination to a fortuitous mistake. Did not stout come about because Arthur Guinness burned the hops? So it is with Cream Crackers. George N. Jacob one day in 1885 put the wrong mixture in the machine and came up with the famous layered cracker. Unfortunately, the truth is a little more prosaic.

From 1880 a new type of biscuit began to appear in Ireland. It was relatively plain, but crisp and ideally suited as a base for morsels of savoury food such as cheese or cold meat. The new biscuits had been invented in America and were called crackers. According to notes left by Charles E. Jacob, the first crackers to be marketed in Ireland were Niagra Crackers, made by a manufacturer known as Marsh and Company, probably an American firm. Then another cracker from an American company known as Larrabee came onto the Irish market. Jacob's looked upon the new arrival with concern as they were very popular. In 1884, Jacob's began to produce its own crackers, called Canadian Crackers, to counter the competition.

However, it was felt that a more serious response was called for and, in the same year, George N. Jacob was dispatched to America to investigate the situation in the cradle of the cracker, as it were. He arrived home armed with the know-how to produce a cracker that would leave its rivals far behind. Experiments were carried out, and, a cracker called Wave Crest, was launched, which, although it survived until the 1930s, was not a raging success. However, in 1885, a new recipe and process were tried and Cream Crackers were launched. The new crackers, a Jacob's original, were an instant success, and quickly became the company's best-seller, as they remain to this day. The early experiments took place in a brick reel oven of the type George had seen in America. This did not meet with success and the travelling ovens were used instead. The reel oven was put to other uses however, and indeed was in use in the factory until after the Second World War. Another consequence of George's visit to the United States was the installation of a sprinkler system, which he had seen in factories there.

FURTHER EXPANSION

The establishment of a limited company meant that shareholders had to be informed of the firm's progress. The second annual report showed a profit of £7,229, with a dividend of 12% paid out, leaving a balance of £1,229 to be brought forward to the next year's account. By 1891, profits had risen to £16,902 and a 20% dividend was being paid. In the following year, the company's capital was increased from £75,000 to £100,000 by the creation of 250 preference shares of £100 each. A reserve fund was set up, and from it £10,000 was invested in railway stock in 1896.

The new responsibility to shareholders spurred the company to expand sales, and importation of English biscuits into Ireland saw a counter-offensive by Jacob's. As early as 1886, a commercial traveller, Mr Badcock, was appointed in London and achieved sales of £1,400 in his first year; a depot was established in Liverpool in the same year. Albert Jacob was sent to look after business there, and became a prominent citizen of that city. Unlike his father and brothers in Dublin, Albert entered public life. He became a Liberal councillor for the Aigburth Ward in 1906, a position he held until 1912 when he resigned. By 1892, there were twelve travellers in England. In 1894, the company targeted new districts in the north and midland counties of England. The lower dividend to shareholders that year was explained by the expense incurred in opening up these new markets in the face of stiff competition from English and Scottish manufacturers, and some loss was experienced at first. By 1896, a reduction in the price of biscuits was seen owing to the continuing competition in the market place. In 1902 a depot was opened in London and in 1906 another at Trafford Park, Manchester.

In 1893, a notable sale was made. A telegram was received from Berlin addressed to 'Jacob's England' ordering six tins of Cream Crackers for Prince Frederick Leopold – a tribute to the international fame of the Dublin snack. In January 1899, the workforce stood at 1,346. However it must be remembered that this was after the Christmas rush had subsided – there would have been many more seasonal workers employed two weeks before.

Many Quaker industrialists were unsympathetic to advertising, finding its exaggerated claims contrary to the spirit of George Fox. They preferred the old-fashioned promotion of their products by allowing their quality and pureness to speak for themselves. Indeed, in a time when adulteration of food was widespread, the public put their trust in Quaker-produced food items. However, times were changing and eventually Quaker firms were forced to take to 'puffing' their merchandise like everyone else. However, the message did not quite reach Bishop Street. In 1905 Jacob's set aside £1,500 for advertising. This compares with the £69,000, £119,000 and £127,000 spent on their advertising budgets by the Quaker firms of Fry, Cadbury and Rowntree respectively in 1910. However, promotional displays were occasionally mounted. A sum of £500 was spent on a stand at the Dublin International Exhibition of 1907, on the site of what is now Herbert Park, Ballsbridge.

DEATH OF WILLIAM JACOB; OPENING OF LIVERPOOL FACTORY

During these years, William Jacob continued to direct the enterprise, but gradually began to pass the business on to his sons. William lived for many years in Ballybrack House, Military Road, Killiney, a large early eighteenth century house of three bays in a beautiful secluded setting. William remained Chairman until his death at the Portobello Nursing Home on 5 August, 1902. For one of Dublin's greatest industrialists, the event was barely noticed in the Dublin press. William Jacob had lived a quiet, modest life, never seeking the limelight, as was the Quaker tradition, and he died as he had lived. He is buried beside his wife in the beautiful Friend's burial ground in Temple Hill, Blackrock, Dublin, surrounded by his fellow Quakers. Unlike his father, his resting place is marked by a headstone. It is exactly like all the others in the burial ground, simple and dignified. William died a rich man. In his will he left £82,327 4s. 8d. to three of his sons George, Albert and Charles. The youngest son, Henry William, became a medical doctor, and from 1902 until his death in 1928, researched the early history of the family, the results of which were privately published in 1929.

Following the expansion of the business in England, a momentous decision was made when it was decided to set up a manufacturing base

Grave of William Beale Jacob and his wife, Hannah, in the Quaker burial ground, Temple Hill, Blackrock, Co. Dublin.

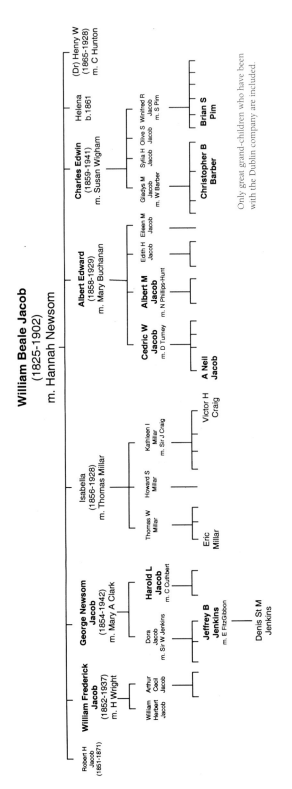

Descendants of William Beale Jacob. Those marked in bold type worked in the company.

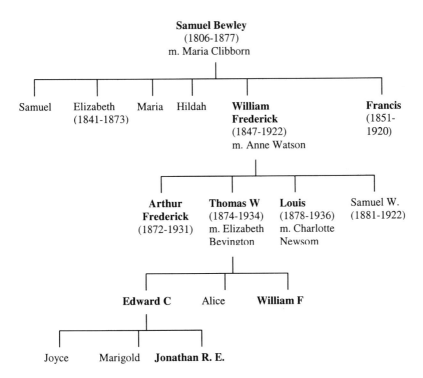

Samuel Bewley
(1806-1877)
m. Maria Clibborn

Samuel | Elizabeth (1841-1873) | Maria | Hildah | **William Frederick** (1847-1922) m. Anne Watson | **Francis** (1851-1920)

Arthur Frederick (1872-1931) | **Thomas W** (1874-1934) m. Elizabeth Bevington | **Louis** (1878-1936) m. Charlotte Newsom | Samuel W. (1881-1922)

Edward C | Alice | **William F**

Joyce | Marigold | **Jonathan R. E.**

Descendants of Samuel Bewley. Those marked in bold type worked in the company.

in England. The inability to expand production owing to lack of space in Bishop Street to meet the growing export market was a major reason for the move. Expensive night-work had been introduced to meet demand and there was a desire to eliminate this. The uncertainty caused by the possible introduction of Irish Home Rule may also have been a factor. Not surprisingly, the site chosen for the new factory was Liverpool, where Albert was based and the Jacob name well-known. Labour was plentiful and a suitable site was found at Aintree. It was near the great port of Liverpool, with a direct shipping link to Dublin and had excellent rail and road communications with the rest of Britain.

By 1912 the first factory block was completed and production commenced. Technical staff was sent over from Dublin to help the launching of the Liverpool factory. To help Albert, his two sons, Cedric and Maitland, together with W. Denis Hunton, a great-nephew of G. J. Newsom also went over to assist.

In the same year as the opening of the Liverpool plant, the Dublin factory made an important contribution to biscuit-making technology with the installation of the first gas-fired travelling oven. This method of baking was soon taken up by the biscuit industry generally.

1913: INDUSTRIAL UPHEAVAL

In 1910 and again in August 1911 there were outbreaks of industrial unrest at Jacob's, especially among the younger males and the bakehouse girls. A reason for this perhaps can be seen in the wage structure of the bakehouse at this time. An analysis of the strike at Jacob's by Patricia McCaffrey[1] shows that the largest single group of women was that working alongside the men in the bakehouse. She has estimated that 66.7% of the women in Jacob's earned between seven and ten shillings a week. Although the minimum pay could be as little as 4s. to 4s. 6d. a week, very few actually earned this as most of them were on piece-work which boosted their earnings. An interesting comparison can be made between the earnings of those known as bakehouse men No. 1 (older male workers), bakehouse men No. 2 (mostly young men and boys) and bakehouse girls. The average wage for the older men in a week in August 1913 was 28s. 7d.; for the young men and boys 12s. 2d. and for the girls only 8s. 2d. It must be borne in mind however that it was commonly felt at the time that it was men who earned for the support of the family and that the earnings of women and girls were

---

1.   Patricia McCaffrey, 'Jacob's Women Workers During the 1913 Lockout', *Saothar* 13.

William B. Jacob

Founder and First
Chairman

George N. Jacob
Second Chairman

Charles E. Jacob
Third Chairman

SONS OF THE FOUNDER

H. Lansell Jacob
Fourth Chairman

A. Maitland Jacob
Fifth Chairman

GRANDSONS OF THE FOUNDER

Edward C. Bewley
Sixth Chairman
Grandson of William F. Bewley
who joined the business in 1864.

Jeffery B. Jenkins
Deputy Chairman
A great-grandson of the founder.

JOINT MANAGING DIRECTORS

Jacob's chairmen up to 1960.

seen as welcome contributions to the family income; they were not intended to make them independent.

James Larkin personally helped to settle the 1911 dispute and was thanked by George Jacob for his efforts. For its part, Larkin's union, the Irish Transport and General Workers' Union (ITGWU), agreed to give forty-eight hours notice of any intended strike and Jacob's began to increase wages. Larkin issued a handbill urging the workers to abide by the agreement. However, relations soon turned sour between the labour movement and Jacob's. The *Irish Worker,* Larkin's newspaper, began a sustained campaign against the Jacob's management. The paper scoffed at the Quaker sentiments of the Jacobs, who it claimed 'purport to run the business for love', and only keep the factory open to give employment to the poor.

By August 1913, as a result of large-scale union activity by Larkin and James Connolly and the opposition of employers, industrial relations in Dublin were on the point of open warfare. Jacob's did not escape. As the great lock-out began to take hold of the city, tensions were raised in Jacob's when George Jacob sacked the secretary of the No. 2 branch of the ITGWU, a man by the name of Gibson, for being in a pub. Gibson then began to organise union activity from the uncomfortably close 77 Aungier Street.

By the morning of Saturday, August 30, 1913, tension was high between Jacob's management and members of the ITGWU. Shortly before half past twelve, a consignment of flour from Shackleton's Mill in Lucan arrived at Jacob's. A few days before, Shackleton's, owned by a Quaker family, had locked out members of the ITGWU working at the mill. As a result of this, the goods of Shackleton were 'blacked' by the union. Three men working in the mixing loft of Jacob's refused to handle the flour and were dismissed. However, it was now near the closing time of 1 o'clock and most workers went home without hearing of what had happened. Also that morning, a regulation forbidding the wearing of trade union badges in the factory was issued. George Jacob later claimed that the wearing of union badges was an attempt by women union members to intimidate non-union workers. He claimed that such intimidation, in other forms, had been going on for some time.

On the following Monday, 1 September, management instructed workers that all goods, including those from firms that were locking out members of the ITGWU, were to be handled. This led to large-scale defiance by workers and 670 of the 1,059 male workers and about 300 of the females decided not to work. Management then completely closed the factory, stating that only workers renouncing the ITGWU would be reinstated: technically many of the Jacob's female workers belonged to the Irish Women Workers' Union, run by Larkin's sister, Delia, but in reality it was a section of the ITGWU.

This action led to Jacob's goods themselves being blacked. Dockers at the North Wall refused to handle Jacob's skips being loaded on the London and North Western Railway's steamer *Snowdon*. Over one hundred workers of the railway then walked out in support of the dockers. Two weeks later the factory re-opened with a gradual build-up of a non-

ITGWU workforce – first males then females. To get the bakehouse working, a small number of men were brought over from the Liverpool factory and the Manchester depot. Returning workers were required to sign a form renouncing the ITGWU.

On 11 October, Jacob's issued an ultimatum stating that those workers who had not returned to work by 15 October would be taken off the firm's books. The firm rewarded those who braved the insults of their fellow-workers who were on strike by giving them an increase of one shilling in their wages to women and two shillings to men – this was known as loyalty money. When most of the Dublin employers rejected the report of the Dublin strike inquiry published on 14 October 1913, attitudes hardened on both the side of the employers and of those still on strike. As many Jacob's workers lived nearby, those locked out were usually found on the streets surrounding the factory. This led to many disturbances and, on a couple of occasions, full-scale riots. On 3 November a serious fracas took place between Jacob's workers still on strike and those working. Women workers were chased by strikers through the grounds of St. Peter's churchyard and attacked all the way down George's Street.

A minor *cause célebre* arose out of the many cases of intimidation and physical assault on workers by strikers. This concerned a young Jacob's striker called Mary E. Murphy. Murphy was charged with assaulting one of the girls who had returned to work, while she was on her way to the factory on the morning of 3 November 1913, by giving her a box in the

FORM OF AGREEMENT.

I PROMISE that while I am in the employment of W. & R. JACOB & CO., Ltd., I will not belong to or support The Irish Transport and General Workers' Union.

I ALSO PROMISE to give One Week's Notice before joining any Strike, and will give my Employers every opportunity, before doing so, to investigate any grievance.

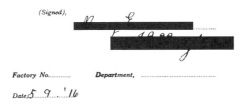

(Signed),

Factory No............   Department, ...

Date,5.....9......'16

Form of agreement required to be signed by employees renouncing the Irish Transport and General Workers' Union; as can be seen it was being signed as late as 1916.

face and calling her a 'scab'. She acted in a similar manner that same afternoon when the girl was going back to work after her dinner. The case would have been forgotten about among the numerous other similar cases that were happening all over the city had not Murphy been remanded for a week in High Park Reformatory, Drumcondra, on a site which also housed a Magdalen Asylum. Murphy was subsequently charged with assault and sentenced to one month's imprisonment in the same reformatory. She had not been sent to prison like the rest of her fellow activists because she was under-age – she was variously described as fifteen and sixteen. The reformatory was a place of detention under the Children's Act of 1908.

James Larkin was also imprisoned at this time and a campaign was begun by the labour movement to have him and the other labour prisoners released. Larkin was freed having served less than three weeks of a seven-month sentence. On the evening after the release of Larkin, James Connolly, speaking outside Liberty Hall, informed the throng that a 'young girl who had been sentenced in connection with the strike had been removed from Mountjoy to an institution at Drumcondra for fallen women'. He appealed to the 'custodians of public morality' – the clergy – 'if they had any shame left', to denounce the detention in every pulpit on Sunday. He went on to say that if they did not denounce 'this damnable outrage they would be whited sepulchres and hypocrites'.

The press picked up what they saw as Connolly's attack on the clergy and questioned as to whether the girl was actually in the Magdalen asylum or not. The anti-union side claimed that there were two separate institutions, the reformatory and the Magdalen asylum, on the one site and that Murphy was in the reformatory and had no contact with the home for fallen women. The labour side pointed out that the two institutions were on the one site and run by the same order of nuns, and that the inmates of the asylum and the reformatory were in sight of each other in the chapel, and that this was a scandal. The case led to letters in the newspapers and demonstrations, including one planned for the convent itself, but it was stopped by the police when the 800 protesters had reached Fairview. The matter was quickly forgotten when Murphy was eventually released.[2]

There is no doubt that George Jacob took a hard line with workers during the lock-out, and in the early months of 1914 the Jacob's women were

---

2.   For the full story of this incident see Peter Murray, 'A Militant Among the Magdalens: Mary Ellen Murphy', *Saothar* 20.

the last large group of workers still locked out in the city. The matter came to an end in May 1914 when Jacob's management, still refusing to take ITGWU members back *en bloc*, agreed to consider individual names presented to it by the union's solicitors as vacancies arose. The dispute caused much bitterness and bad publicity for the firm at the time. Jacob's management attempted to counter this by inviting church leaders, local authority representatives and the press into the factory to see conditions and the level of welfare enjoyed by the workers.

Before leaving this period, mention should be made of Rosie Hackett, a woman, associated with Jacob's, who is worthy of note in labour history. Rosie was a young messenger when she joined the ITGWU in 1909. When the union called a strike in Jacob's for better pay and conditions the following year, Rosie was an enthusiastic supporter of what turned out to be successful action as far as the workers were concerned. Rosie was active again in the 1913 lockout, especially in Liberty Hall, helping to feed workers' families. Rosie was not taken back to work after the lockout. She was active in the formation of the Irish Women Workers' Union and fought with Michael Mallin in St. Stephen's Green in the 1916 Rising. Rosie died in 1976 after a lifetime commitment to trade union activism.

The 1914 Jacob's financial report shows a significant reduction in profits due to the 'sympathetic strike'. They were down by £10,246 from the previous year's level of £45,167. It reported that overall about half the workforce had joined the strike, but that their places were gradually filled up, mostly by new applicants. During the period required to train the new employees, the company faced a considerable loss. The loss in trading amounted to two months, and during that period all travellers, clerks and salaried officials were paid in full. Other costs were incurred by the necessity of sending and receiving goods by circuitous routes. For this, motor vehicles had to be employed by the company – perhaps for the first time. Both the factory and a premises on New Row had to be guarded at night and on Sundays by a large force of employees. What was described as 'the volunteer staff from Liverpool and Manchester' had to be housed and boarded for several months. Legal action was taken against the 'National Labour Press' for circulating a pamphlet of an anti-Jacob's speech by Larkin. An apology was widely circulated, but at Jacob's expense.

WAR AND REBELLION

The company had hardly time to recover after the lockout when its production was seriously hit by the outbreak of the Great War. Raw materials such as sugar became difficult to obtain and a scaling back in the making of more fancy biscuits was necessary. This was offset to some extent by a demand for plain biscuits by army canteens both in Ireland and abroad. The demand for sweet biscuits fell anyway as the public responded to appeals for austerity in support of the war effort. Army canteens were supplied with biscuits in packets. In the two final years of the war Jacob's were supplying over 1,200,000 packets of biscuits a week to the canteens.

During the period from August, 1914 to October, 1918, a total of 388 men from the Dublin factory enlisted in the British army. Of these, twenty-six were killed and a large number wounded. From the Aintree factory and the English depots, 262 enlisted or received commissions and twenty-six were killed and many wounded. The firm regularly sent cakes or tins of biscuits to its employees serving overseas. In November 1914, the Dublin factory loaned a 4-ton Leyland lorry to the Red Cross for despatch to the front in France, where it served in the early months of the war when motor vehicles were in short supply.

It is doubtful if any of the Dublin men fighting in the trenches ever dreamed that war would soon come to their native city, and indeed, to their place of employment in Bishop Street. The Irish Citizen Army, led by James Connolly, which arose from the ashes of the lockout, together with the Irish Volunteers, decided that it was imperative to strike against England while that country was distracted by war in Europe. Easter 1916 was set as the time for a rebellion. The plan was to hold Dublin city centre for as long as possible against the vastly superior forces of the British army, in the hope that the rest of the country would follow the rebels' example and rise.

In order to achieve this, it was necessary to defend the main arteries into the city centre, and so prevent enemy soldiers entering it from the

4-ton Leyland lorry lent by the company to the Red Cross in World War I.

A 6-ton load of biscuits for the troops in World War I.

battery of British army barracks that surrounded Dublin, or from the port of Kingstown (Dún Laoghaire). The intention was to seize a number of easily-fortified positions commanding the main routes to the city. Jacob's biscuit factory presented such a fortress commanding the route from Portobello Barracks, Rathmines along Camden Street and Aungier Street into the city.

Easter Monday, 24 April, 1916 was a Bank Holiday, and, as usually happened on such occasions, it was arranged that a small number of Jacob's workers would turn up for work to carry out maintenance of various kinds which could not otherwise be done while the machinery was in motion. These included fitters, firemen, boilermen and outside chimney sweeps who had come in to undertake a job.

Some time between twelve noon and one o'clock that afternoon, a group of 150 men, some armed, broke into the factory on the Bishop Street side. They were commanded by Thomas McDonagh and included Con Colbert and Major John McBride. The following account found in Jacob's archives of the events of that historic week is based on statements made by three employees in the factory. The rebels immediately proceeded directly up the stairs to the top of the building, as if they knew where they were going. A group of workers immediately informed the caretaker, Thomas Orr, and the watchman on duty, Henry Fitzgerald, of the invasion. They immediately phoned George N. Jacob, who was the chairman of the company at the time and one of the managers, Mr Dawson. The communication was made just in time, for moments later the telephone wires in the whole area were cut. Despite the disruption in the city, they managed to arrive at the factory after some time. While this was taking place, one of the volunteer officers collected all the workers and placed them under a guard, at the same time placing a guard at the principal entrances.

Typical packets of biscuits (left) for the troops in World War I; the variety known as Verdun was particularly popular. In World War I Jacob's tin-making department ceased normal production but 150,000 mess tins of this type (right) were made for the troops at the front.

After a short time it was decided to allow all the workers to leave the factory, which they did. Thomas Orr takes up the story:

> The watchman came to me and asked me what he was to do; I advised him to go home with the others, I taking possession of his clock and keys. During his absence for his coat and hat, I was told to leave, which I at once refused to do. I explained that I was caretaker, and no matter what was the result, I could not leave (which they afterwards admired me for), and they moreover told me that in case of an invasion by the military, we were just in as dangerous a position as they were. Well, as I remarked, the watchman had gone for his clothes; when he arrived back the hall door was barricaded and he was detained a prisoner with myself. They then took possession of my apartments and remained there until Sunday 30 April. Fortunately my family had gone for a day's pleasure.

The rebels had four other prisoners with them, including two detectives of the Dublin Metropolitan Police, whom they had detained at the premises of Barmack's in New Row.

The rebels went about securing the building by erecting barricades at weak points with all sorts of material, of which a plentiful supply was always on hand. Every available vessel was filled with water and left in a cool place in case the city water supply was cut off.

The watchman, Fitzgerald, was questioned by McBride as to his name, religion and address and, having answered, he was asked to allow himself to 'be sworn in as a member of the Sinn Féin Volunteers'. He stated that he was never a member of any organisation, political or otherwise, and that all he wanted was to be released and allowed to go home to his wife and children. 'This answer seemed to cause disappointment', he reflected afterwards.

During their occupation, Orr made three appeals to the rebels, two were granted and one refused. He appealed to the Commandant (McDonagh) to prevent smoking in the factory as far as possible, and he immediately issued orders for smoking to cease. The second appeal concerned fourteen horses that were not being attended to. They were stabled a little distance from the factory itself and each time they needed attention the barricades had to be removed. At first McDonagh agreed to the request, however, when he saw how much potential danger this involved he became reluctant to allow the operation to take place. Orr then requested that he be allowed communicate with George Jacob to see if the horses could be removed, but this was refused. However, whenever the horses were in real danger, McDonagh always allowed them be seen to.

On Tuesday of Easter Week, very early in the morning, several rebels were sent out to obtain provisions. At about eight o'clock they arrived back with the contents of two bread vans, which had just left their bakery, and a large quantity of milk, beef, mutton, bacon and many kinds of tinned food. They also had a quantity of boots and the contents of McEvoy's stores on Redmond's Hill, and Larkin's tobacco and chandlery stores, Wexford Street. On the same day, clergymen were admitted to hear confessions and absolve every man, as the rebels expected an attack any moment.

Spirits among the rebels were high and they were sure of victory. However, on Wednesday the mood began to change. That evening a rumour spread that the staff in the Adelaide Hospital were removing all the patients to the back of the hospital to allow the military to occupy the front. Orr stated that if the rumour were true, the rebels would have destroyed the hospital by fire using the large supply of bombs that they had.

On Wednesday, the rebels asked to be shown where the printing plant was, as they wished to snipe at Dublin Castle. At 11 p.m. the occupation of the factory set off the fire alarm which operated a sprinkler. Fitzgerald was aware of the vast quantity of flour that would be destroyed. When he pointed this out to the rebels, they had the water turned off by a plumber they had with them in case repairs were needed.

Orr stated that 'the watchman and myself were sick of listening to their boasts of victory', such as that British money was of no value anymore as their military had been defeated in all directions; or that Holland had proclaimed war on England and France had quit the war, and that was

During World War I, an N.C.O. sent the company this picture of troops using a Jacob's
biscuit box as a table in the Lybian desert. The group suggested the title 'Chums' and
Jacob's produced an assortment under this name suitable for relatives and friends to send
to the troops.

why Russian troops were brought over to France 'and all such nonsense
as this'.

Fitzgerald and Orr were asked to peel potatoes, but they refused, and
the two D.M.P. detectives were forced to do so. Fitzgerald and Orr got ill
during the week due to inhaling gases and sulphur and 'the bad sleeping
arrangements'. There was no doctor available, only a chemist, and the
two prisoners refused to take medicine from him as they feared that it
might not be the correct one.

By Thursday it was clear to Orr, by the demeanour of the officers, that
things were not proceeding satisfactorily outside, but that the men in
general were full of hope, for they were, he claimed, kept in the dark as
to what was happening. The rebel headquarters in the factory were in the
clerks' cloakroom. On Friday, two clergymen from Church St. came to
the factory and were brought to the cloakroom on what appeared to Orr
to be some sort of peace mission, for shortly afterwards McDonagh left
the factory and held consultations somewhere outside.

On Saturday morning, a cycle company went out on some mission,
but returned after twenty minutes very frightened, and one of them, a
man by the name of O'Grady, was severely wounded. He was brought to
headquarters and 'examined by a man who was supposed to be a doctor,
but whom I think was only a chemist' repeated Orr. After examining him
he ordered him to be seen at once by a priest, and to be brought over to
the Adelaide Hospital, where he died about 4 o'clock in the evening.

As a result of negotiations, an unconditional surrender was signed by McDonagh and others and read aloud to all the men on Sunday at 2.30 p.m. They were told that they had only an hour to leave the premises. This came as a great surprise to many. Orr saw some of them burst into tears and others break their rifles and revolvers on the ground in rage, saying that they had been duped and sacrificed themselves for nothing. In the end, however, they saw that there was nothing for it but to retire, which they did in four different sections.

Orr went on to say in his statement that during the whole time of occupation he never saw anyone under the influence of drink or using bad language. He stated:

> Let me now conclude by saying that but for the sudden collapse, and the influence brought to bear on them by the clergy, it would have been a difficult matter to remove them from the factory. I was afraid they would have destroyed some of the machinery, but Providence altered their plans. Things could have been much worse, and I am quite certain that the majority of the employees are thankful today for the turn events took.

When leaving, Con Colbert shook hands with Orr, who asked him where he should go. Colbert told him that he could go to hell!

Another employee, Peter Cushen, takes up the story from the time of the rebels' surrender on Sunday 30 April. Having heard of the surrender, Cushen hurried down to the factory to observe what was happening. He saw about ninety rebels emerging from the factory windows and 'the rabble' getting up the rope that was hanging from the office window, and tumbling out sacks of flour. He ran round to the caretaker's door in Peter Street and got into the bakehouse, where he was surprised to see what he estimated was between 90 and 100 of the rebels standing and sitting about.

He then made his way through them to the office, and caught up a rifle from the floor, where there were many of them lying around. With this he attempted to drive the looters out, but more were getting in through other windows and he was unable to keep them all out. Just then help arrived:

> Young Johnston, Pat Barry, Tom Doyle, Bill Kelly, McGrath, P. McEvoy and others came and took up old rifles, and we stopped the looting for the time being. Then one of the officers of the rebels came into the office, and asked me if there was anyone to take charge of the place,

and they told him that I would. He said there was a lot of bombs stored away that would blow up the whole place, and as they had done no damage, they did not want the blame to be left on them if any careless person handled them. He brought me round and pointed them out to me, and we came back again and he showed me where there some hand grenades stored in the little ovens in the King's Own Room (King's Own was a variety of biscuit); he left me on guard of them and told me on peril of my life not to let anyone lay a hand on them until the military came in who knew what they were. He then went away after making himself known to me, and to my surprise, I found myself introduced to Major McBride for the first and last time, as we all know he paid for his mad acts with his life.

Well, he was not well done when a volley of shots rang out all round about where I was standing, and the 2" Sprinkler Main over my head was pierced through with a bullet, and the hat was knocked off my head by a bomb fired through the open window. Luckily for me it passed through a window and exploded over the refrigerator outside. Well, I thought my last hour had come. Just then the soldiers came in and shouted 'hands up', and up they went in haste; then they came over and searched me, asked who I was and what had me there. I told them I was an employee of the firm and that I came in to stop the looting. They said 'If you are a member of the works, you know where the d— rebel flag is hanging out, and get on to it at the point of the bayonet'. I said 'you are not one bit more eager to get it down than I myself, but before I go I want to show you these weapons of danger – the bombs'. Then we started on our way to the flag-staff, and went to three or four doors but could not get in the way they were barricaded. At last we got in through the cake room and away to the tower; I would not let him get out for fear of the snipers, but I got the rope and lowered the flag and no sooner than it began to come down than 5 or 6 shots rang out – I do not think that man could have been prouder if he was after taking the Empire of Germany!

On their way back, Cushen was told by the soldier that he was a lucky man that he had nothing in his hands when he came in or he would have shot him where he was standing. When they got back, Fr. Aloysius of Church Street and Fr. Monaghan of Francis Street arrived and went to the British officer in charge and told him his troops were not to stay about the place as orders from the Castle stated that no soldiers were to appear on the scene until six o'clock, when the volunteers had departed.

However, when the military left, the looting began again. This time the looters managed to break the panels in the office door and there were

VIEW OF W. & R. JACOB & CO.'S EXHIBIT (Grand Central Palace, East Wing), showing Working Model at right side of Picture.

A Great Attraction!

Working Model of a
. . . Biscuit Factory.

W. & R. Jacob & Co., Ltd.,

Invite attention to their Stall, situated in the Large Central Hall, close to the Band Stand. The Models have been made in the Engineering Department of the Biscuit Factory, and accurately represent the intricate machinery necessary for the production of High-class Biscuits.

(Above) Jacob's stand at the Irish International Exhibition of 1907 on the grounds of what is now Herbert Park, Dublin. The glass-framed model of a biscuit-making machine is now in the Civic Museum, Dublin: (below) Invitation to Jacob's stand at the 1907 Exhibition.

so many involved that Cushen and his men were powerless to stop them. Cushen sent for Fr. Aloysius, who came up and waded through eight inches of water to the window, and made a speech to the crowd outside, telling them they were a disgrace to the city. This had the desired effect and caused a lull for a while. Cushen then got all the hands to barricade the windows with all the tables and sheet iron that they could lay their hands on. They then went down to No. 9 oven and neutralised eighteen hand-made bombs by placing them in the water tank in the wash-house.

As soon as they had this done, they saw nine or ten lads at the end of No. 9 hoist. They were pursued and ran through 'Dan O'Malley's workshop' where another group of about nine looters were manhandling bags of sugar out through the window. The looters were put to flight and this window barricaded also. When they had everywhere secured and the factory ready for occupation by the military, they departed through the Peter's Row Gate and down Peter Street. However, Tom Doyle went up Peter's Row and was shot at the corner of Digges' Street. Cushen concluded his account 'so ended the siege of Jacob's Fort'!

In 1961, at an exhibition night held by the Old Dublin Society, two burnt biscuits were displayed. It was said that they were made in Jacob's factory by some young volunteers who could not resist making them during Easter week despite being told not to touch machinery. They were burnt to a cinder, but the company name was still legible.

An interesting survivor of the occupation of Jacob's was John McDonagh, brother of Thomas, who had fought under his brother in the factory, and was sentenced to life imprisonment. He had been a well-known opera singer in the United States and around the world when the call to arms came. He was a captain in the volunteers. After his release from jail, he went back to America and wrote a Broadway play *The Irish Jew* about the election of a Jew as Lord Mayor of Dublin. With so many Jews and Irish in New York, it was a big success and ran for years. He returned to Ireland and became director of productions in Radio Éireann. He wrote many more plays, composed songs and was a pioneer in the making of Irish films.

Another noteworthy volunteer in Jacob's was Michael J. Molloy, the printer of the proclamation of the Irish Republic. He had mobilised outside the College of Surgeons at 11 a.m. on Easter Monday morning and marched to Jacob's under McDonagh. He was later a compositor for many years with Independent Newspapers.

The company's annual report of 1917 states that production resumed in the factory after four or five days' clearing up. About 100 bombs were left behind by the rebels in various parts of the factory, but no damage was done by them. Compensation for looting was paid by the government. With the ending of the Great War, full working capacity returned to the factory in 1919, when supplies of raw material such as sugar were reported to be back to the 1915 level.

CHAPTER THREE

The Figs in the Fig Rolls

The making of biscuits on an industrial scale requires huge amounts of food ingredients from home and abroad. Visitors to Jacob's biscuit factory in Bishop Street were fascinated to discover that the making and baking of biscuits was done on the same principles that their mothers used in their kitchens at home, but on a gigantic scale. The mixing was carried out from well-tried recipes, and the mixers were for all the world like those used in the home but of cement mixer dimensions. Indeed Jacob's worked from recipe books just like the housewife. Some of these books survive from as far back as 1898. Here are some of the ingredients for a trial recipe for Cocoanut (Jacob's spelling) Macaroon from 1934:

28 lb.	Flour
140 lb.	Cocoanut
76 lb.	Sugar
1 quart	Syrup

A new Pixie mix was made the following year. Ingredients included:

12 st.	Progress flour
3 st.	Rice
65 lb.	Fine sugar
30 lb	No 1 Butter
36 lb	Nucotine
2 lb	Full cream milk powder
4 lb	Separated milk powder
2 3/4 gal.	Water
1 glass	Butter flavour
1 glass	Egg yellow

The finest produce of the Irish countryside was selected by Jacob's to make their famous baked confections, in particular, wheat flour and dairy products. Flour was carefully selected. Boland's, the Dublin millers, and Odlum's were amongst the suppliers of Irish flour. Odlum's, an old milling firm, owned the Leinster Flour Mills, Naas, which were established in 1791 and remodelled in 1921, as well as mills at Sallins, Portarlington and Saint Mullins. Shortly before the move to Tallaght in the 1970s, the Bishop Street plant was using sixty-five to seventy tons of flour each day. Native flour was not suitable for some biscuits, notably Cream Crackers, which needed extra-dry, hard flour. This flour was imported from Canada and later from Europe. Flour came to Bishop Street in sacks loaded on lorries. When they arrived, the sacks were carried on conveyors from the street level to the Flour Loft, where they were stored. The father of Luke Kelly, the Dublin balladeer, worked on the Flour Loft. His work entailed lifting the sacks off the conveyor and storing them. Workers remember the high Flour Loft, where the windows were usually kept open, as the coldest part of the factory.

Many creameries and dairies were patronised by Jacob's for the large supply of milk and eggs needed each day. The richness of fresh milk and cream was constantly to the fore in biscuit names, for example Club Milk. In the 1950s, churns of milk arrived each day at 4 o'clock and butter came, in 56 lb wooden boxes, from various Irish creameries. Different varieties of butter were supplied, as some biscuits required soft butter and some hard. Big rolls of cheese were also delivered for use in savoury biscuits. Like the flour, sugar also came in sacks. A tractor and trailer regularly went to the Dublin railway stations to pick up the sacks which had been despatched from the Irish Sugar Company. Mollasses was also obtained from the same source. Some sugar was further processed by Jacob's, by grinding it to produce icing-sugar. The laboratory constantly screened arriving raw materials for purity before they were put to use. Samples from each new delivery were tested, a forerunner of modern traceability.

Imported materials, either ready for use or to be processed in Ireland, consisted of cocoa beans from Africa and America, and fruit (including cherries, currants, sultanas and figs) from France, Spain, Portugal, Greece, Cyprus and Turkey. Dessicated coconut came from Ceylon, and ginger from various countries in Asia. Fats extracted from such sources as palm, rape seed and beef oil were also imported. However, the latter fat was gradually phased out and only vegetable oil used.

The flour first went to the Mixing Room, where the mixing and kneading machines incorporated other ingredients to produce a dough of the required quality and texture. By the 1950s, dough was mixed in a battery of high-speed machines, each capable of mixing three-quarters of a ton in ten minutes, using push-button control and automatic timing. The mixture was moved about in dough wagons and pushed by a man to the machine. The dough was then tipped from a dough wagon elevator, fifteen feet in height and capable of lifting ten hundredweight at a time onto the rolling and cutting machines. As one worker reminisced 'you

Flour being delivered in the 1930s; the conveyors can be seen in the background.

would really need a horse to move them'. The rolling machines rolled the dough in endless sheets to acquire the requisite thickness. It was then cut into the shapes needed. Dies, punches or moulds shaped it into circles, ovals, rectangles, squares, and other shapes so familiar in house-holds everywhere.

The ovens were in the Bakehouse, which was on the ground floor. Men came in very early in the morning, at 4.30 or 5 a.m., to get the ovens hot for the day's baking. Those working on crackers also had an early start. The 'brakesmen' who rolled out the dough could be in at 2 o'clock in the morning so that it was ready for the machinery at 8 o'clock. The raw dough shapes then entered a long travelling oven on metal trays carried on conveyor chains. The shaped dough then moved through the ovens at the pace required for just the right length of time for that particular type of biscuit. The baked shapes then emerged brown and crisp ready for packing, or proceeding to other departments where they were trans-formed into chocolate biscuits, cream sandwiches or iced or decorated varieties. The ovens were originally fired by solid fuel, but, as already noted, in 1912 the first gas-ovens in the industry were installed in Bishop Street by W. J. Purdy, a joint general manager of the firm.

CHOCOLATE-ENROBED BISCUITS

Considering the Quaker association with chocolate in Fry's, Cadbury's and Rowntree's, it is not surprising that Jacob's began to make its own chocolate. This luxurious, indulgent and indeed, sensuous food product has its origins in the mysterious traditions of the Olmec and Maya of the New World, where it was indulged in as a drink. Brought to Europe under great secrecy by the Spanish, it was originally imbibed only by the wealthy. It became popular among all as a drink after 1828 when a Dutch chemist, Coenraad Van Houten, invented a revolutionary extraction process. The original drink was very oily, but Van Houten's hydraulic press succeeded in extracting about fifty per cent of the cocoa butter present in the liquid. Having separated the butter from the bean, a question arose as to what to do with it – it was too good to be thrown away. The Fry family in England began to process it and market it as a snack food in solid form. And so chocolate was turned from a beverage into a confectionery.

Chocolate-making was a very important part of the work of Jacob's. The company took great pride in the quality of its chocolate biscuits and great care was taken in the complicated chocolate-making process. Indeed, one old employee remembered the Chocolate House as being almost a separate factory. 'There were really three factories in one: the Biscuit Factory, the Chocolate Factory and the Tin Factory' as he put it. In Bishop Street, the huge sacks of cocoa beans amounting to many tons arrived once a year from South America. They were brought to a store-room where they were kept cool; they had to be turned every few days and moved from pallet to pallet to keep them well-aired, and were carefully dusted to avoid any loss of condition.

A process of selection, grading, roasting and blending took place to turn the cocoa beans into what is known as chocolate 'couverture' to coat biscuits. Roasting brings out the flavour and enriches the colour of the chocolate. The degree of roasting was carefully controlled as too much created a bitter taste. The beans were then cracked open and the shells or husks removed. During World War II, Jacob's sold the shells from which people made their own cocoa drink, and it was much sought after among a public starved of hot beverages as a result of rationing. The cocoa-oil or butter was then squeezed out of the beans. The residue was ground and mixed with sugar. Then some of the cocoa butter was put back, and careful blending took place. This process required knowledge of the characteristic flavours of the different beans and was acquired from long years of experience. After blending, the liquid chocolate was carefully refined to ensure smoothness in a machine

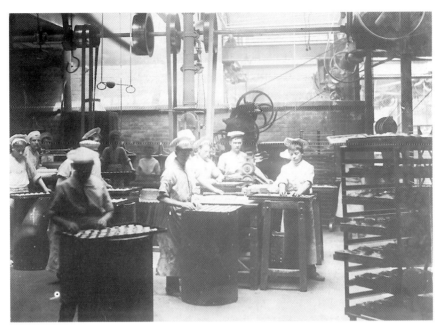

Boys preparing biscuits for the oven 1898.

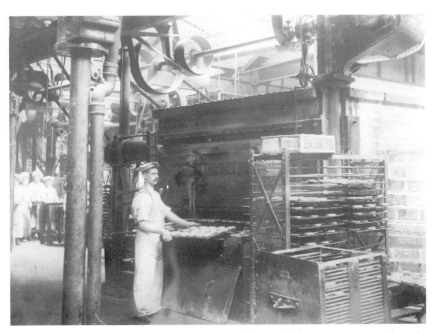

Oven 1898; Jacob's always employed a number of master bakers to oversee work at the ovens.

known as a 'Conche'. This process could take several days. The conch-
ing machine agitated the liquid in order to further enrich the flavours of
the chocolate and allow it to mellow and reduce the residual bitterness.
At this stage, various flavours, such as vanilla were added. The refined
velvety liquid was then pumped through heated pipes to the enrobing
or moulding plant where biscuits of many kinds were covered with both
plain and milk chocolate. In an automatic and continuous process, the
chocolate biscuits then passed through a cooling chamber where they
were set to a hard attractive glassy finish.

Chocolate-making at Jacob's was discontinued in 1961, as it became
increasingly difficult to attain the required volume. For a while, chocolate for biscuits was bought in blocks from Urney's of Tallaght, Co.
Dublin and melted down in the factory. However, in 1962 Urney's were
able to provide liquid chocolate. To receive this liquid, tanks were
installed in Bishop Street. This is one of the first jobs Jonathan Bewley,
the son of Edward C. Bewley, remembers working on as a young engineer. Today, bought-in chocolate is stored at the Tallaght plant in liquid
form in huge tanks fitted with giant stirrers.

As it became common to take snacks in all sorts of places, and indeed
while on the move in an increasingly mobile society, individually
wrapped biscuits became popular. In 1901, Jacob's launched their biscuit bars which developed into the famous Club variety. These were
chocolate-coated biscuits, attractively wrapped, bearing names associated
with various leisure pursuits. In an advertising poster designed by W. H.
Barriball around 1925, a society 'flapper' in an orange robe and high-heel
shoes of the period is perched on a buffet-table languidly indulging in a
coffee and a Jacob's Club biscuit. Varieties included Theatre Chocolate
and Cinema Chocolate, reflecting the huge popularity of the new silent
Hollywood films. Sport was represented by Cycling, Golf, Hockey, Soccer
and even Cup Tie, and Mashie for knowledgable golfers. The flapper of
the poster is probably nibbling on a Charleston bar in its blue wrapper
depicting in silhouette a couple dancing the night away. The star of the
series was Club Milk itself, thankfully still with us. The original wrapper
featured the King of Clubs from a deck of cards, so the idea was to asso-
ciate the luxury bar with the camaraderie of a card-game or the glamour
of London's clubland. Flavour-based varieties included Orange and
Nougat Milk. Added to these later were Nutana and Sultana.

Coconut arrived in Bishop Street from the Phillipines and Sri Lanka,
and figs came in blocks from Turkey. How the latter are inserted into the
famous Fig Rolls is, however, covered in a veil of secrecy! However, the

CHRISTMAS CAKE
(Oval)
A rich fruit cake with almond icing;
nicely ornamented. Made in two sizes
Approximate weights—
1 lb. 10 ozs. and 2 lb. 10 ozs.

WALNUT CAKE
A sandwich cake with chocolate-
flavoured icing; decorated with
white icing and walnuts

NOEL CAKE
A popular fruit cake with attractive
ornamentation, as illustrated
Made in two sizes
Approximate weights—
1 lb. 5 ozs. and 2 lbs. 5 ozs.

CHRISTMAS CAKES FOR CHILDREN
A delicious cake, iced with soft sugar and prettily decorated;
made specially for children and packed in an attractive
enamelled tin suitable for Christmas Stockings

JACOB & CO'S CAKES

As well as biscuits, Jacob's Christmas cakes were very popular.

ENAMELLED TINS

TEA CADDY
A beautiful and useful casket
packed with rich biscuits

BRISTOL CHINA CASKET
A dainty and artistic box,
suitable for cigarettes or
trinkets, containing an assortment of rich biscuits

JACOB & CO'S
ENAMELLED TINS

Elaborate and fanciful tins were kept as ornaments long after their contents were eaten.

Oriental-style tin label.

Fancy biscuits were associated with the world of glamour and luxury;
in this case the theatre land of the West End.

confectioner's art was seen at its most perfect in the Marshmallow Room, where creams of many colours and flavours were applied to the biscuits before they emerged as marshmallow creams of all varieties. The spongy, luscious confection known as marshmallow was first produced by Jacob's in 1897. Before World War II, marshmallow varieties included, besides the ever-popular Mikado and Kimberley, such exotic delights as Regal Mallow, Columbo and Fruit Cream.

Biscuit names can evoke the spirit of the times in which they were first baked. Mikado conjures up the colourful oriental world of the Gilbert and Sullivan opera, while Kimberley captures the glamour of South African diamonds or perhaps stirring events in the Boer War. Biscuit names tend to be generic. Even names always associated by Irish people with Jacob's such as Marie and Marietta were available from other manufacturers. However, Cream Crackers of course were a Jacob's invention, as also were Puff Cracknel, introduced in 1897, and the variety called Wave Crest, previously mentioned.

Icing of biscuits was carried on in a separate department. One pensioner remembers that as a lad new to the factory this was in the charge of a formidable lady:

> men were not allowed put their nose inside the door. She was very strict. She would ask you what you were doing there. Each department wore different coloured overalls at the time and she would know where you were from. The company never realised how conscientious the workers were.

Before the 1960s, icing and creaming (the sandwiching of biscuits) were done by hand by scores of girls working at large tables. Applying mallow and cream was known as piping. The biscuits were then cooled and sprayed by hand with a coating of sugar or coconut. Cream sandwich biscuits included Custard Creams, Kerry Creams and, a childhood favourite of the the author, Creamy Chocolate. Singing while you worked was encouraged by the management and teams of girls often worked to the rhythm of a popular song of the day to help allay the monotony of repetitive tasks. One ex-employee remembers one whole section of girls rhythmically creaming biscuits to the recitation of the Rosary, at the instigation of a particularly pious supervisor!

Before World War II, Jacob's were producing up to two hundred varieties of biscuit. The afternoon tea-drinker of the twenties and thirties had a bewildering choice of individual dainties and exciting assortments to choose from. War-time shortages and increased mechanisation streamlined the range to around sixty different lines. While the after-noon tea market was always in mind, a special assortment of confiseries known as Afternoon Tea Confections, consisting of small rich cakes and petits fours was specifically designed for that market. Some biscuits, such as digestives, were marketed for their health-giving qualities. Jacob's Nu-Vita were described as 'an invigorating and sustaining food containing natural vitimins essential to good health'. They were pro-moted as nourishing and easily digested and an ideal substitute for toast. Rusks for the nursery were also produced. They contained vitamin D which Jacob's introduced into the biscuit by acquiring the rights of what was known as the 'Steenbock process'. These were recommended for young children and invalids for the prevention of rickets, still a prob-lem before World War II. 'Kinder Garten' biscuits were still being pro-duced for small children. They were in the shape of the letters of the alphabet.

Finished biscuits, not immediately packaged, were placed by women in wooden boxes called 'whippets', which were made by the factory car-penters. Packing tins was labour-intensive and required some skill. It was carried out by women with a picture of the arrangement of the assort-ment required before them. A pre-World War I account romantically describes the preparation in the packing rooms of biscuits for export to many parts of the globe, especially the far-flung corners of the empire:

> Here in these packing-rooms I see what a world-field Jacob's Biscuits have conquered. They are popular in Continental and Colonial house-holds, notwithstanding the biscuits made in those countries. Here cases to be carried across the forests and mountains of Asia are being shipped to Rangoon. Here others are being soldered in air-tight cases to be safeguarded against the white ant and enjoyed in South African or American ranches; some are being given a dainty lemon flavour to satisfy the Asiatic palate. Most curious of all, some vast sheet-iron water-tanks, each standing five feet square, and destined for the Far East, are being filled with biscuits, so securing economical carriage, each of them holding twelve to eighteen hundredweight. The cases sent to the English depots at London, Liverpool and Manchester are even more colossal.

The water tanks must have been greatly welcomed in the remote des-tinations to which they were dispatched.

It is not commonly known nowadays that Jacob's made more than bis-cuits. A 1930s catalogue lists wedding cakes, family cocoa, pastry flakes

Packing biscuits for export before World War II.

Biscuits setting out for exotic destinations all over the world.

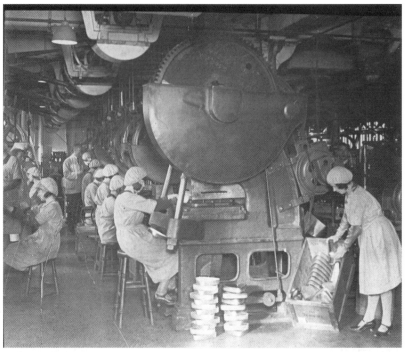

Making tins.

Labelling large tins.

(Above) A Tennant & Ruttle Commer van delivering Jacob's chocolates in 1958. (Below) An undated photograph of a Jacob's delivery van in Bishop Street.

and chocolate confectionery. The Cake Department was described as a big cage-like structure where such mouth-watering varieties as Arabian Cake, a soft cream sandwich containing vanilla and orange, Colleen, a popular fruit cake, and Waverley, containing cherries, sultanas and other fruit, were baked. Also available were Ginger and Madeira Cake, Lemon and Jam Sandwiches and Oxford Lunch. Rich bracks were also produced.

Cakes were baked for the Christmas market. Jacob's rich wedding cakes were always very popular. A Princess Wedding Cake could be purchased for 1s. 10d. per pound. It could be embellished with ornaments and floral decorations also available from Jacob's. A number of the expert icers in the Cake Department did a side-line in icing cakes at home to order.

CONFECTIONERY – SWEETS AND BARS
From 1926, Jacob's began to experiment with the production of chocolate confectionery. The experiments proved successful and plant for the making of confectionery, including chocolate sweets and bars, was established at the Bride Street end of the factory in 1930. In 1933, Jacob's purchased an interest in the distribution firm of Tennant and Ruttle and allocated its confectionery lines to it for distribution. This innovation coincided with the accession of Fianna Fáil to power and the imposition of protective tarrifs which greatly affected the confectionery trade. Many British companies such as Fry-Cadbury and Rowntree-Mackintosh set up factories in Dublin, and Jacob's entry into the market came at the right time.

Chocolate sweets produced by Jacob's included Patricia chocolates, Rich Milk, and Chocolate Peppermint Creams. Virginia Bars, beloved of many a child now above middle-age, were also a firm favourite. Easter eggs were also made.

Experimentation was always going on. A memo from the factory floor from October 1934 states: 'Please note that it has been decided to alter the recipe of the Teddy Bar, increasing the malt by a half pound in the nougat, and reducing the butter from 3 lbs. to 2 lbs. and adding 1 lb. to the Nucoa'. In relation to the same bar, another memo from 1935 reveals that a certain amount of market research was being conducted:

> Teddy Bar – please note that the centre containing brown sugar is much preferred by the majority who have been asked to give an opinion.

Another note from 1938 states: 'Honibar – we are now prepared to go ahead with this new line'. In July 1933 a problem with a trade name arose: "Crisp" – this name in all cases will from today take the place of "Crunch", the latter word being registered in the name of Synnott, Capel Street, Dublin. Please make whatever alterations may be necessary in your department'.

Jacob's gave up the production of confectionery at the end of 1961. With the arrival of competition in the form of Boland's, Jacob's felt the need to concentrate on its core biscuit business and required the space in Bishop's Street. Apart from the valuable space taken up by plant, the confectionery had to be stored for a month before dispatch as the centres of the chocolates had to liquify. Also, the confectionery machinery was aging and replacement would be costly. The turnover on confectionery, only £60,000 in 1960, did not justify such an expense.

In the tradition of the young Robert Jacob, sales representatives blazed the trail for Jacob's biscuits around the country before World War II. The son of one such traveller remembers that Jacob's representatives were regarded on the road as the elite of commercial travellers. They received the best of attention at country hotels and in the evening could often be found with other representatives of top companies dining at a special table. As the mass-market in consumer goods underwent a revolution in the nineteenth and twentieth centuries, the importance of presentation of commodities was realised.

For most of their history, biscuits were sold loose and selected and weighed for the customer by the friendly and trusted local shopkeeper. The biscuits were displayed in attractively-labelled tin boxes. The labelling was even more important when, on special occasions, especially Christmas, the housewife would be expected to splash out on such a luxury as a whole or half tin of biscuits.

By the 1870s, decorated tins for special occasions were becoming popular. The designs grew increasingly complex and by the 1890s, tins were often shaped to look like real-life objects, such as suitcases, carriages, books and postboxes. The tins kept the biscuits fresh, and could be kept as attractive decorative accessories, or as toys in the case of those tins designed with children in mind. Christmas was the busiest time of year, and novelty tins helped to increase trade at this time. Biscuits presented in these cleverly designed tins were the perfect gift. Tins were just one element in merchandising campaigns, other point-of-sale material included signs, posters and shop displays. The biscuit companies also promoted their products through advertising in newspapers and magazines. Trade cards were distributed as well as such novelty items as pocket mirrors, puzzles and pamphlets. Promotional miniature tins were also distributed as stocking fillers at Christmas; for instance, Huntley & Palmer's, the biggest biscuit manufacturer in Britain, distributed miniature gramophone records.

The son of Joseph Huntley, the biscuit-maker, also Joseph, started Huntley, Bourne and Steven's, the first biscuit tin-making factory, to supply his father's firm. Business expanded and they began to make tins for many manufacturers, including Jacob's. Biscuits packed in decorative tins continued to be big business through the early part of the twentieth century, although production was slow to pick up following World War I. The approaching World War II and the need for metal, as well as the loss of workers to the war effort, spelled the gradual demise of fanciful biscuit tins. However, this has been revived in recent years, although the designs are not as fanciful.

Jacob's tin-making plant was originally based in the Bishop Street factory but moved to the old Dunlop's tyre factory in St. Stephen Street, close to the biscuit factory. This is an historic building in itself as it housed the works of John Boyd Dunlop, the inventor of the pneumatic tyre. He opened the first pneumatic tyre factory here at No. 75 in 1889. Tractors and trailers collected blocks of tin, up to twenty tons at a time, from the North Wall.

Each year, Jacob's drew the attention of its shopkeeper customers to its latest range of enamelled tins. Such tins where the printing was applied directly to the metal were never made in Bishop Street but were ordered from Huntley, Bourne and Stevens or the Ashtown Tin Box Company, Castleknock, Dublin.

For the 1938 Christmas market, Jacob's offered a very handsome tea caddy of rich lacquer, red and gold in design, filled with a 'particularly good mix'. For children, in addition to an attractive range of miniature tins, they offered a humming top filled with biscuits. They explained this as 'an entirely original idea, and as it will be a source of amusement long after the biscuits have been consumed, we feel that there will be a very big demand for it'.

Tins were moved around the Bishop Street plant on wooden bogies, which made a very distinctive sound as they moved on their small wheels over the steel floors. Jacob's discontinued making tins about 1963. An internal conveyor system created by Cyril Fry, the maker of the Fry model railway, now on display in Malahide Castle, Co. Dublin, was also in use. Cyril Fry trained as a railway engineer at Broadstone, Dublin and worked there and in Inchicore for twenty years before he took up a post as engineer in Jacob's in 1943. He earned fame for his model transport system, consisting of trains and trams, that he built in his home in Churchtown, Dublin. Indeed, his whole house was a veritable transport museum, starting at the hall and leading to his famous model railway in the attic. His transport system in Jacob's consisted of canvas conveyors that carried goods around the factory.

Jacob's put much thought, creativity and artistic endeavour into the labelling of tins. Up to the 1960s tins had paper labels attached, both on

DUBLIN TO FLORIDA

"BISCUITS UPON THE WATERS."

Messrs. W. & R. Jacob & Co., Ltd., have just received the following interesting letter at their factory in Bishop Street, Dublin :—

Delray Beach, Florida,
August 6th, 1928.

Messrs. W. & R. Jacob,
Dublin, Ireland.

Dear Sirs,

Perhaps it will interest you to know that I have just found a tin of your biscuits washed up on the beach at Gulf Stream, near Delray Beach, Florida. The tin was without wrapper or label and somewhat rusted. My husband opened it, and we were surely surprised at the condition of the contents. The dainty biscuits were deliciously fresh and crisp, perfectly packed, not one broken in the least. It is truly wonderful after being dashed about in the rough ocean for weeks – or perhaps months.

I am keeping the tin for a souvenir—but the biscuits are "taking wings."

Sincerely yours,

(Signed) Mrs. LLOYD D. PERKINS.

Extract from a Dublin newspaper, 22nd Aug., 1928.

the lid and on the sides. The use of a trade mark or logo goes back to the 1930s. An original design for a special tin of Teatime Assorted, by an artist named Freda Beard, was obtained in 1922 from the Baynard Press. From this the famous 'Trumpeter' trade mark evolved. A collection of tin labels, beautifully printed in full colour by the Printing Department, and worthy of an exhibition, is held by the company. The company also made its own corrugated paper that was used to separate biscuits before the days of plastic trays.

The Printing Department was established in 1900. It turned out millions of labels and packet wrappers as well as stationery, price lists and publicity material. In the 1960s, Heidelburg printing presses were in use and a Chambon five colour photogravure machine could handle paper and a wide variety of materials then being used for packaging, including vegetable parchment, cellulose film, and laminated paper which would be heat-sealed for protection. The department also did printing for outside customers. An invitation to the celebration of the twenty-fifth anniversary of the establishment of the printing section survives.

Workers were invited on a charabanc outing to Powerscourt waterfall, to be followed by a function in the Powerscourt Arms Hotel in Enniskerry. Printing was discontinued in Bishop Street before the end of the 1960s. The printers, belonging to an ancient craft, regarded themselves as an elite, and even had a separate entrance.

In the 1930s, biscuits were sold to retailers in either square or small tins. The square tins contained a nominal 10 lb. of biscuits and the small tins half that. Tins for export contained up to 28lb. Prices were quoted per hundredweight so the customer would have to work out how much his order cost using the ready reckoner printed on the price list. Thin Arrowroot for instance cost 115s. per hundredweight loose, while made up in half pound packets they cost 125s. per hundredweight. There were five varieties of ginger biscuit: Ginger Dingles, ginger-flavoured finger biscuits; Ginger Buttons, described as small and round; Ginger Snaps and Ginger Nuts, both described as round and sweet; and Ginger Wafers, round and thin. Some of the most exotically-named biscuits were Dixie Crackers, Hurling, Ratafia, Colombo and Corinth. Irish placenames were invoked in Kerry Creams, Avoca Creams and Donegals.

As well as the tins, half-penny and farthing biscuits could be purchased in wooden boxes and cardboard containers. Fifty-four farthing biscuits could be purchased for a shilling, leaving the shopkeeper with a profit of one and a half pence when the box was empty. Glass lids to fit square and half-square tins to facilitate display could be obtained, supplied with hinges, at two shillings each. When goods were sent by rail or steamer, the company paid carriage on orders to the value of two pounds or over. Accounts were due when the goods were furnished.

Empties were returned to Jacob's, where the old labels were removed and they were were steam-cleaned and sterilised, and, where necessary, reconditioned before being used again. Eventually a huge washing plant with automatic control was installed for this. Those who knew it, remember this plant as an unpleasant place in which to work. It was necessarily noisy, hot and wet. The girls who worked there wore wooden clogs because of the damp. A deposit, depending on size, of 2s. or 1s. 6d. was charged on tins. An old Cocktail Assorted tin still held by the company indicates that an extra effort at recycling was made in war time. It has a paper label attached to the side bearing the legend: 'Save metal – 2d. refunded for this tin if returned in good condition to W. & R. Jacob and Company'. On 31 December 1926, the company estimated that there were 682,772 tins in customers' hands costing 1s. 6d. each. They were concerned with the small number being returned in any one year, and

Jacob's van preparing to take part in the 1958 St. Patrick's day parade. Driver William Morris (on right) with un-named 'vanboy'.

made a determined effort to recall as many as possible before the deposit on each tin to the customer was reduced to one shilling. In 1952, Jacob's patented a new tin in conjunction with Messrs. Moon Bros. of Birkenhead.

The move away from tins was in evidence as early as the nineteen twenties. An innovation in biscuits was pioneered by Jacob's in this part of the world in 1927. In that year, John P. Fox travelled to the USA and on his return introduced the first air-tight cartons for biscuits not only in Ireland but on this side of the Atlantic. Fox is also credited with introducing air-conditioning in the factory.

DISTRIBUTION

Up to the 1960s, biscuits were mainly distributed by rail, with the retailers picking up their consignment at the rail heads. Large wooden cases were loaded onto horses and drays and transported to the Dublin railway stations. The large wooden cases were made at a Jacob's premises in New Row, where large nailing machines were constantly in operation. Jacob's had some vans for city deliveries. Chassis were bought in and a team of coachbuilders was employed to build vans on them in a premises in New Street. Sign-writers were employed to paint the distinctive Trumpeter sign on their sides. With the increased cost of rail transport and better roads and road vehicles, a fleet of vans was built up and by 1966, country deliveries were being carried out in these. Supplying the Jacob's depot in Belfast for the distribution of biscuits in Northern Ireland was a vital part of the supply network. For many years, in good times and bad, this task, regarded as dangerous at times, was carried out by driver John Doyle. Every day, resplendent in special drivers' uniform, he crossed the border; he became so well known that on his last trip a special party was held for him in the customs post. For the city, small vans and messenger boys on bicycles were used. Many shopkeepers came in their own cars to the Town Office to collect orders (a Country Office dealt with orders from outside Dublin). A well-known personality in the Town Office was Miss Rose O'Brien, who retired in 1962, having joined the firm in 1915. To many city shopkeepers and messenger boys she was 'Miss Jacob's', a title bestowed on many other ladies before and since.

'THE BEST JOBS IN DUBLIN' – WELFARE IN JACOB'S
'Jacob's and Guinness's were the two best jobs in Dublin' was the opinion of a male Jacob's worker who started work in Bishop Street in the 1950s at £7. 15s. a week. At that time a batch of seven or eight young lads were called together. They were first brought to the surgery for a medical examination, and having passed that, they started work.

An early form of 'clocking-in' existed. A 1918 handbook for male employees informed the men and boys that each male employee should have a metal check with his number stamped on it which must be put on the board when arriving in the morning and also after dinner. This had to be done by each worker himself – on no account was a colleague to do it for him. If the check was lost, an employee had to pay two pence to have it replaced. It further stated that no pins were to be worn on clothing. Most serious of all, chewing tobacco, and, reassuringly, spitting, were forbidden on pain of dismissal. Health and safety was a priority even then. Wages were dispensed to each worker at the end of the week in a small round tin with his or her number on it and the tin handed back.

Jacob's workers wore aprons and caps as protective garments. These were purchased by the employees and had to be laundered in their own homes. In the early years of the twentieth century, the first laundry and sewing room were built and these were upgraded in 1934. They were eventually situated at the junction of Peter's Row and Peter Street, on the site of a well-known public house called Kenny's, which Jacob's had taken over. The sewing room made the protective clothes, such as white coats

Office interior 1898 .

used on the factory floor. In 1960, the space was needed for increased production and the service was given to Swanline Service, a subsidiary of the Swan Laundry, experts in such work, and so the company was relieved of laundering. The company believed that 'the better service and more varied colours would increase the morale of the employees'. The new arrangement would, it was claimed, result in a cost reduction of up to 15%. Employees had to pay a small weekly amount to defray the cost of the service.

Both permanent and temporary workers were employed in Jacob's depending on the trading conditions or season. A note from J. P. Fox in October 1936 stated that before permanent workers were moved from one department to another, any temporary workers should be moved first. It was also pointed out that no permanent worker should earn less money owing to the presence of a temporary worker. An internal memo from 1932 stated that girls working to 7 p.m. should be allowed go to the Girls' Dining Room for ten minutes for a cup of tea if they desired. A five-day week was established in 1938. From September or October on, to cope with the Christmas demand, a special 'Married Womens' Shift', known in the factory as the 'Granny Shift' worked between 6 and 10 p.m. It was illegal to employ women after this time at night. Workers remember these women being kept separate from the young girls as they might 'talk about subjects unsuitable for young girls'. This was the only exception to the marriage ban in Jacob's whereby women had to leave work when they took on the responsibility of a husband and family. Girls were occasionally dismissed for 'immorality': that is becoming pregnant. Before being shown the door, they were given a stiff lecture on the foolishness of their actions causing them to lose one of the best jobs in Dublin. One ex-employee witnessed one such lecture being given to a girl by a very strict and formidable supervisor. Just as the unfortunate girl was about to leave the room for the last time she had the temerity to ask to speak. Taken somewhat aback, the senior lady gave her permission. 'You can be sure it will never happen to you', the girl boldly stated and shut the door behind her.

The marriage ban greatly affected the workforce. One ex-staff member remembers that in 1950 out of a total of forty women working in the offices twenty-six left that year to get married, including herself. However, chinks were appearing in the system; because they were short-staffed they were forced to take three back. Turnover in staff must have created problems, as at that time it took seven months to train women to use the new Powers-Samas technology installed in the offices in 1958–9. This system automatically calculated, checked and printed invoices on the punched card system. It was state of the art at the time and a constant stream of personnel from other firms in Ireland visited Jacob's to investigate it. This was a first step in the automation of invoicing, which had previously been done by hand.

At ownership and managerial level, Jacob's was very much a dynasty, and a parallel situation existed among workers. In 1961, a journalist spoke to five young workers whose great-grand-parents had worked in the factory when it opened in 1851. 'My great-grandfather, my grandfather, my father, mother and three aunts have all worked here', said Rita Collins proudly. A twenty-year-old electrician, Edward Bolger, had a similar story to tell: 'My great-grandfather was the first time-keeper here. Since then my grandfather and grandmother and my father have all "clocked in"'. Two sisters, Agnes and Kathleen Woods, said that their grandmother, Mary Grubb, was one of the first employees in the company. Her starting wage was 3s. 6d. a week; their minimum wage was four guineas, and more if they did piece-work.

Working hours for the general workers in the factory were from 8 a.m. to 6 p.m. up to the 1960s. Employees known as 'staff' worked in the offices or at management level. Before World War II, the normal working hours were 9 to 5.45 for office staff and 8 to 6 for the managerial staff in the factory. Juniors were taken on a three-month probation. Regulations pointed out to these juniors that smoking was permitted on the garden roof during lunch hour and at certain specified times in the Staff Dining Room. To encourage thrift, a savings' bank and a holiday fund existed. Broken biscuits could be purchased on Mondays and Fridays and a library was in operation in the waiting room of the Girls' Welfare Department.

Mary (May) Sherman, who died recently at the age of 106, and started working in Bishop Street in January 1908, remembered the Jacob family fondly, although her details of who exactly was who were inaccurate:

> It was lovely, there was a grand crowd in it, and the Jacobs themselves were lovely men. There was Mr Charles, there was Mr George, and there was Mr Albert. Now Mr Albert was over in the Aintree factory in Liverpool. Mr Charles had two daughters, Gladys and the youngest girl was Sylvie, and Mr George had one son and his name was Edward. And all the Bewleys: there was a big family of Bewley's there. There was Mr Fred, Mr Frank, Mr Louis, Mr Arthur and Mr Tom. I was in the print-

Engineering Shop.

ing room. I was at the book-folding for the price lists for Liverpool.

May had memories of events of great historical importance: 'I remember the rebellion and I remember the Great War (of) 1914, and I had a brother killed there and he worked in Jacob's'. She explained that while many of her colleagues went on strike in 1913, she did not – her mother would not allow her! She married on the 4th of June 1927. On leaving Jacob's she got a wedding cake, two pounds, and a dinner service from the Printing Department.

Dan Dent and Billy McDonagh worked in latter years in Bishop Street. They remember that you were regarded as lucky if you had a permanent job on a machine. They explained how the 'line system' worked. With such a huge workforce there could be up to a hundred people absent on any given day, so it was important to have a reserve of workers who could be sent where needed:

> If you were not on a machine or the machine you were on was down, you had to go to the line. On the line you could be sent anywhere, to the Bakehouse, Chocolate house, sent on the vans. Different departments would send down for two or three men or boys. There were huge crowds on the line. If say nine or ten were left after all the jobs had been given out, they would be sent to the cleaning staff. You could end up on the roof with the cleaning staff. You were on a wage

Girls' Dining Room.

– no one was ever sent home because there was no work.

Before this, the line formed outside in Peter's Row for men looking for work for the day. A team of men and boys from the line would be used to deal with big jobs that arose from time to time, for instance, if a shipment of cocoa beans came in and needed to be unloaded. Women were never on the line. Nowadays, 'the line' refers to the ovens.

Many boys started work at the age of fourteen and were let go at nineteen. Only a certain amount of males were kept on after this age. As a worker remembered:

> There were many more women than men. The women were not long in the factory when they were sent up to the third level where the packing school was to train. Some women worked bringing messages from one department to another all day. The women did all the packing, and men operated the machines and lifted the heavy boxes for the women onto bogies.

Jacob's Swimming Pool; adjacent to the Bakehouse, it proved popular with employees working in the hot environment on warm summer days.

The Engineering Department was responsible for the smooth running of the factory's plant. Jacob's engineers pioneered many innovations in biscuit-making technology. Much of this was forced on them by the very cramped nature of the Bishop Street premises. An example of the creativity of the Jacob's engineers was the installation of sloped travelling ovens. The factory was not long enough to install ovens of the length required. The engineers came up with the idea of circumventing this by sloping the ovens, despite the conventional engineering wisdom that this could not be done. The principle objection was that the heat would all lodge at the highest end of the oven. However, the Jacob's engineers got round the problem by a series of fans ensuring equal heat, and the ovens worked to perfection. An interesting event took place in September 1962: Leslie Forsyth, chief engineer at Jacob's, retired and was succeeded by Henry P. Mowatt; the company took the opportunity to present a large model of biscuit-making machinery to the Dublin Civic Museum, where it still remains, but unfortunately is not on display to the public. In the early 1960s, mechanisation greatly increased, ending much of the tedious and labour-intensive manual work.

Quaker firms in England pioneered workers' welfare. By 1888, Jacob's were supplying refreshment for its workers by having milk on sale in the factory, and in 1891 a coffee bar was established as well as dining rooms. At the turn of the twentieth century, the dining room and kitchen were

An interview with the Jacob's doctor.

found on the upper part of the premises. About 750 workers dined in the dining room every day. What was described as 'a good meat dinner' could be obtained for twopence, the workers sitting on long benches with tables in front, all facing in the same direction in regimented style. However, all was not constraint; a piano was provided for a 'sing-song' afterwards and a library was situated nearby. By the 1920s, prices had risen as one ex-employee recalled: 'We had a dining room and you could have your dinner there every day, a lovely dinner for sixpence.'

On the roof was a spacious recreation ground and garden, where, it was reported, 'from this breezy height we enjoy a sea-breeze and a view of the Wicklow Mountains and the hills around Dublin'. Photographs published in the *Daily Mirror* in an attempt to offset the bad publicity of the 1913 lockout show a group of girls in white aprons in a large circle dancing to the applause of their fellow-workers.

Jacob's installed a swimming pool in the Bishop Street premises, an amenity unique to any company in Ireland, and rare even today. There was also a recreation hall with provision for games such as badminton and table-tennis. An athletic ground upon which cricket, football and pitch and putt were played was situated in Rutland Avenue, Crumlin. A gala occasion took place every year (and, indeed, still does) when the Dublin and Liverpool factories played each other in football. The first Jacob's choir was founded in 1909, and classes were held in first aid, languages, sewing and handicrafts. A Social and Entertainment Committee with members drawn from all sections of the company organised excursions twice a year; Killarney, Galway, Bangor and the Isle of Man being very popular. In addition to these events, fashion shows, question times and demonstrations of beauty culture were also organised.

The first factory doctor, George P. Cope, was appointed in Jacob's on a part-time basis in 1894 and a dentist in 1907. All doctors worked a certain number of days at fixed times; at one stage there were two. A welfare department was set up in 1906 and a savings' scheme inaugurated. A Co-Operative Guild was also set up by workers and provided vouchers for shops which could be paid back interest-free. These facilities were an attempt to keep workers out of the clutches of moneylenders, then very active in Dublin. The factory came to all but a standstill in the first two weeks in August for the annual summer holidays. Production ceased but repair work was carried out and deliveries continued.

The medical facilities consisted of a waiting room, doctor's rooms, surgery, dentist's surgery, rest room, with the office of the superintendent and welfare secretary nearby. Medical attention was free, the only

TELEGRAPHIC ADDRESS:
"JACOB, DUBLIN".
TELEPHONE N.º 2588 (2 LINES)

BY ROYAL
APPOINTMENT

TO H.M.
THE KING.

ORIGINAL MAKERS OF
CREAM CRACKERS.
PUFF CRACKNELS, ETC.

W. & R. Jacob & Co. Ltd

BISCUIT & CAKE
MANUFACTURERS.
ESTABLISHED 1851.

DEPÔTS:
LONDON, DOCKHEAD, S.E.
LIVERPOOL, 286, SCOTLAND RD
MANCHESTER, TRAFFORD PARK.
SALE ROOM 21, FENNEL ST.

BISHOP STREET,
Dublin, 28th January 1916

Please quote Reference *Lilie O'Connor*
27 Constitution Hill

We send you the Wedding Cake herewith as an expression of our appreciation of your services whilst in our employment, & we hope that the time spent with us has been a pleasant & helpful one to you.

We would like you to know that you carry with you our good wishes for a very happy married life, & we hope that you may be comfortably settled in your new home.

We do not like completely to lose sight of our girls when they leave us, & wish them to feel that we still have an interest in their welfare, so that if you will write to someone here after a while, & let us know how you are getting on, we should be very pleased to hear from you. When writing, mention your maiden name & Department worked in.

If at any time you should want advice or information about your health or household matters, Miss Ormiston or any of the other ladies would be very glad to give you any assistance they could.

With best wishes –

W. & R. Jacob & Co. Limited.

No 2 Packets

Letter sent to female employee on her marriage in 1916, expressing a caring, if somewhat paternalistic, attitude. 'No 2 Packets' was the department in which Lilie O'Connor worked. (letter courtesy Bob Monks).

charge being that of twopence if medicine was required. Beds for convalescent workers were retained in the Berwick Home in Rathfarnham. The factory dentist was particularly popular. Outside dentists were very stinting with cocaine to kill pain after an extraction or a filling, however, it was reckoned that the factory dentist was liberal with the drug as the company did not want workers to lose time due to a painful gum!

One female employee remembered Jacob's for one thing in particular: 'it was there I got my teeth (made of ivory). And Dentist Smith was the head man in the dental. . . and they had a surgery and the lady doctor was Miss Farrington'. She paid five pounds for her teeth: 'I only gave half at a time and my mother and I kept the other half between us and then I had to pay the other at two shillings a week out of my wages.' Seventy-five years later she was still using them. She went on to explain: 'I lost two and I brought them to a dentist and he said we could make nothing like that now, so he was giving me the plastic ones. I wouldn't take them.'

Comprehensive pension schemes were arranged for all employees and close contact was maintained with retired personnel, the annual Christmas pensioners' party, now run by the Social Club, being attended by hundreds. A number of employees were presented in the board room with long service awards by the Chairman. A special medal was struck for this purpose and is held with pride by many Jacob's workers' families to this day. Later, a watch was presented to those with long service – nowadays it is a crystal biscuit barrel.

The recreation hall, situated in the Molyneux Chapel in Bride Street, hosted a variety of classes and leisure pursuits from concerts to drill classes. The latter were conducted in the early 1900s by a Sergeant Gillespie of the army for both males and females (separately of course). One ex-Jacob's girl explained that Jacob's paid for cookery classes and sewing and 'you got a present at the end'. She volunteered for cooking, sewing and millinery, but no one else attended the millinery class.

Before World War II, a General Workers' Council met regularly to consider matters relating to efficiency and general welfare. Departmental Committees also advised workers on matters of hygiene and health: avoiding strong tea was one memorable hint. Also in the health area, a St. John's Ambulance Brigade was active in the factory for many years.

Workers who started as boys in the 1950s and 1960s in Bishop Street remember finishing work at 4 o'clock on Tuesdays and Thursdays to attend the company's school until 6 o'clock. Mr Taylor was the teacher. He is highly spoken of to this day: 'a great man he was – all the boys loved him' one worker remembered. As well as the usual school subjects, he taught them woodwork, carpentry, and how to play basketball and to swim. The boys had to attend school on Saturday from 9.30 until 12.30. If they failed to attend they were 'brought up' and asked to explain their absence.

As the factory expanded, property was taken over in adjacent streets and before being taken over as part of the plant, Jacob's found itself in

the position of landlord. In 1923 the company was letting sixteen tene-
ment houses in Bride Street, Peter Street, Aungier Street and Lr. Kevin
Street. In 60 Bride Street, for instance, the tenants were Peter Pidgion,
Mary Duignan, John Mates, Mary Sweetman, James Hayes, M. Maguire,
Elen McCormack and George Bell; they paid a weekly rent of from 1s.
6d. to 3s.

Overall, Jacob's provided employment for many Dublin families strug-
gling with poverty. Many lived nearby in housing conditions that were far
from ideal. Indeed, workers who had spent many years employed in
Bishop Street remarked that the working conditions in the factory with
its warmth, hot meals and recreation facilities were often far superior to
conditions at home. As was usual in industry at the time, hours were long
and wages, although characterised by some as low, were steady for most
and greatly welcomed as contributions to the family budget. The paternalistic concern of the Jacob family for their workers ensured a basic
health service and opportunities for limited educational and cultural
advancement denied to many in Dublin at the time.

CHAPTER FOUR

From Family Firm to National Stage

On the establishment of the Irish Free State in 1922, it was decided to split the company, as the factories in Dublin and Liverpool had ended up in separate states. The two companies were to have equal shares and a copy of the Statement of Intent indicates that both companies were also to share equally in the future development of Jacob's trade. This arrangement appears to have worked well, and the Dublin company continued to supply about 40% of its output to the United Kingdom. The first directors of the Liverpool company were George N. Jacob, Chairman and Managing Director, William Frederick Bewley (Managing Director), Albert E. Jacob (Managing Director), Charles E. Jacob, Cedric W. Jacob, A. Maitland Jacob, W. Denis Hunton and G. Arthur Newsom.

There was much overlap of personnel in the directorship of the Liverpool and Dublin companies. A number of changes in management took place in Liverpool in the following years. W. F. Bewley died in 1922 after

A meeting of the board of Jacob's in the 1930s with George N. Jacob in the chair.

nearly 60 years with the firm. Albert Jacob, son of William, died in 1929 and G. A. Newsom in 1933. George N. Jacob retired from the Chairmanship and was succeeded by Charles. He retired in favour of Harold Lansell Jacob, son of George Jacob, who became Chairman in 1937.

The death of Charles Jacob occurred in 1941 and the following year, George N. Jacob, who had been the public face of Jacob's of Dublin for so many years, died as a result of injuries received in a motor accident. On Wednesday, 16 December 1942, his car was in collision with a turf lorry at the corner of Leeson Street and St. Stephen's Green, Dublin. George was thrown from the car and hit a pole. He was taken to hospital in an unconscious state with serious head injuries, and died on the 19 December. He had been educated in the well-known Rathmines School, Dublin and was a member of the Dublin Port and Docks' Board from 1898 to 1902 and was on the board of the British and Irish Steam Packet Company. He was regarded as a hard-liner in the Lock-Out of 1913. In 1926, he became President of Dublin Chamber of Commerce and of the Associated Chambers of Commerce of the Irish Free State in 1928, a position he again held at the time of his death. He also served as Vice-President of the Federation of Chambers of Commerce of the British Empire. He was Vice-President of the Rotunda Hospital and a member of the board of the Meath Hospital. He was fond of travel, and in 1935, at the age of eighty-one, he embarked on a world tour aboard the *Empress of Britain*. The following year, he travelled to New Zealand on behalf of the Federation of Chambers of Commerce of the British Empire. His achievements as biscuit-maker were many, not least being credited with purchasing the first Fig Roll machine in Europe. The biscuit was an American favourite and soon became one of Jacob's best-sellers. He had a life-long interest in craftmanship and engineering and had a workshop set aside to pursue his hobby. He was a keen amateur photographer and was also a pioneer of motoring in Ireland, and had his own car as far back as 1905. He was survived by his son Harold, who was the Chairman of Jacob's, Dublin at the time of his death. His daughter, Dora, married Sir Walter Jenkins.

During World War II, prices were controlled by government order. However, the supply of raw materials, including flour and fuel, became the company's main problem. Only Irish flour was available, which was not suitable for many types of biscuits. A special biscuit using only Irish flour, called Square Meal, was produced and was welcomed by households badly hit by 'Emergency' rationing. Potatoes were used as a substitute for flour in certain types of biscuits. Great ingenuity was required to keep machinery in operation on meagre supplies of fuel, especially from 1942 on. A large gas holder was installed in Bishop Street which was filled at night time when demand from households for gas was low. On the road, Jacob's commercial travellers were reduced to using bus and train in their peregrinations on behalf of the company.

In 1940, the government appealed for volunteers to defend the country in case of attack. Jacob's, together with many other companies, announced that it would grant half pay to employees who joined the defence forces, and would also keep their jobs open for them until the end of the Emergency. Jacob's was one of thirty-two firms that sponsored advertisements in the national press calling on men to enlist. An interesting notice survives informing employees of the arrangement for payment in the event of air raids. It made clear that no payment would be made for time lost due to an air raid warning to anyone who had not clocked in before the warning sounded, either in the morning or at dinner time. On the sounding of an air raid warning, employees could either take shelter on the factory premises or leave to take shelter eleswhere. Those who left the factory had a period of fifteen minutes grace to return before the doors were closed and they were marked absent. If time was lost due to an air raid warning, an opportunity was given to workers to make up a full week of 45 hours either by extension of normal working period or working on Saturdays.

The war isolated the two Jacob's companies. The Dublin factory could not supply Britain and the Liverpool factory was 'zoned' to the north of England. The export trade, built up over many decades with Britain and the Empire countries, especially in areas in the Far East that had no indigenous biscuit industry, was totally disrupted. This valuable trade had continued to be developed by the Dublin factory in the 1920s and 1930s, with up to 6,000 tonnes being exported annually.

During World War II, factory production in Liverpool was switched to army biscuits. Output was prodigious, but a limited production of biscuits for home consumption was kept up. Government departments, Civil Defence units and a number of bombed-out industries found temporary accommodation in the factory complex. The firm was very active in partaking in all aspects of Liverpool's Civil Defence measures. Bomb damage at the Aintree factory was largely confined to broken windows, but depots in Southampton and Birmingham were completely destroyed by enemy action and others suffered minor damage.

The effects of war were felt for some time. However, a response to post-war conditions by the Irish government had a greater long-term

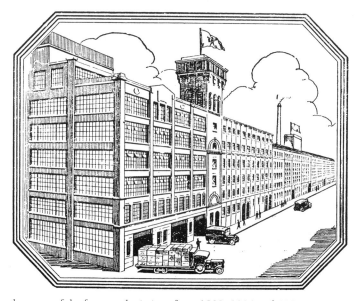

The development of the factory: depictions from 1891, 1904 and 1936.

effect on the Jacob's Dublin operation than anything that had happened in the war itself. In 1948, when the possibility of resuming exports emerged, the Irish government refused Jacob's permission to obtain any ingredients for biscuits intended for sale abroad, due to food shortages at home. The effect of this policy was one of frustration and Gordon Lambert, who had joined the company four years before as a young accountant, expressed the bafflement of him and his colleagues:

> This shortsighted policy stemmed from the fact that we had large agricultural post-war credits; we were living in a fool's paradise of isolation and protection and the need to export seemed irrelevant. . . One can imagine my frustration as the young accountant who had to hand over our export ledger accounts in 1948.

The handing over was, of course, to Jacob's, Liverpool. The post-war years had brought many problems for the English operation. Trade was greatly restricted by way of rationing of ingredients and price control. Rationing hit Jacob's in Liverpool particularly badly. There was a huge demand for biscuits as people wished to put behind them the scarcity and austerity of the war years, but rationing was based on the much smaller pre-war output, so ingredients and other materials were hard to obtain and demand could not be met. For a period, most kinds of biscuits had to be rationed to customers by the company. Shortage of labour was also experienced and this facilitated a trend towards the production of fewer lines.

However, the policy of the British government in relation to exports was the complete opposite to that of the Irish. Despite strict rationing, business was asked to resume as much of the export trade as possible. The attitude of the British government was evident in the fact that it agreed to allocate the quota of ingredients applicable to the world export trade owned by Jacob's of Dublin for biscuits to be manufactured in Liverpool. So in one fell swoop, the huge export trade so painstakingly built up by the Jacob family in Dublin and supplied by Dublin workers over the decades was lost by the city.

Irish distillers suffered under the same restrictions, and this was a large contributory factor to the success of Scotch in the post-war years in America, to the detriment of Irish whiskey.

The new export arrangement coincided with constitutional change in Ireland. In 1948, the new Irish Republic left the British Commonwealth, where most of the export market lay. So perhaps there was a feeling

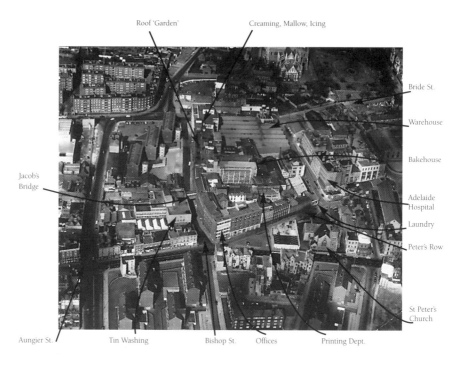

Roof 'Garden'   Creaming, Mallow, Icing

Bride St.

Warehouse

Bakehouse

Jacob's
Bridge

Adelaide
Hospital

Laundry

Peter's Row

St Peter's
Church

Aungier St.   Tin Washing   Bishop St.   Offices   Printing Dept.

Aerial view of the Bishop Street factory.

among the joint Jacob's management that a British company could deal more efficiently with Commonwealth countries. However, the decision had the effect of locking the Dublin firm into the limited home market with very little room for expansion. Also in 1948, the two companies went public and sought quotations on the stock markets.

The period from 1948 to 1956 was a most depressing one for Irish industry. Jacob's, along with other industries, suffered from continued price control, and later even profit control, at a time of relatively high inflation and massive emigration. Growth at Jacob's was stunted and lack of sufficient profits made it almost impossible to replace machinery subject to inflated prices. Certainly, any attempts at planning for modernisation or expansion were out of the question.

In contrast, the Liverpool company expanded in leaps and bounds. Industries in Britain were given incentives to modernise and expand. The Liverpool company took advantage of these incentives to build a separate factory to cater for the expanding Cream Cracker market world-wide. All this had far-reaching repurcussions for the Dublin company. Because of the substantial investment by the Liverpool company in re-establishing the world export trade, the Dublin board was forced to accept restrictive agreements regarding Northern Ireland and the rest of the world, which in effect gave the Liverpool company the right to the Jacob's name outside the Irish Republic.

The early fifties was a period in which Jacob's, together with other Irish industries found itself going nowhere, 'a limbo period' as one senior Jacob's manager who lived through the time remembers. This was in stark contrast to the modernisation that was taking place in British industry.

As the ban on Irish food exports eased, it was agreed with Liverpool that the Dublin company be allowed develop an export market among the Irish abroad, mainly in the United States. This market was never very large. In 1959, Jacob's had agents in New York, Boston, Washington, Chicago and Portland, Oregon; the importer was the Cresca Company of Eighth Avenue, New York.

It is appropriate here to glance at the fortunes of the Aintree factory in these years. When the Liverpool company was formed, the land and buildings were valued at £135,000 and the machinery at £35,000. After World War I, a second block had been added to the factory. One of the great advantages of the Aintree factory over its Dublin counterpart was the fact that it had been built on a green field site and had room to expand.

The distribution system in Britain was re-organised and developed. In Britain, Jacob's had been among the pioneers of direct delivery. Horse-drawn vans were utilised to bring their tins of biscuits via depots to grocers rather than in cases consigned to the rail system for collection at designated stations, as was the situation in Ireland. To the depots in Liverpool, Manchester and London were added premises in Birmingham, Norwich, Southampton, Plymouth, Bristol, Cardiff and Newcastle. In other towns, further storage space was rented. Before long, Jacob's own delivery vans were providing a service from these depots to shops spread over a great part of Britain.

In 1924, Albert Jacob became a member of Parliament and took a lesser role in the work of the factory. He left the business in the hands of his sons, Cedric and Maitland. Cedric Jacob was regarded as a far-sighted manager and the business expanded under his guidance. Like his father, he was a well-known figure in Liverpool and he served with the King's (Liverpool) Regiment. On retiring from the regiment, he devoted much of his time and energy to the welfare of ex-service men in the area. He was also a director of the Liverpool Gas Company. He died in 1937, having been ill for some time. He was succeeded by his son, A. Neil Jacob, who became production director at Aintree in 1947.

The Aintree factory continued to grow. A third block was added in the late 1920s and an air-conditioned building to handle chocolate and sandwich biscuits was built in 1934–35. The administrative offices of the company had been at Scotland Road in Liverpool, but it was felt that it would be advisable to build new offices at Aintree to co-ordinate the production on the one hand and the selling, distribution and administration on the other. In 1928, spacious new offices were erected at Aintree.

ARRIVAL OF BOLAND'S

The biscuit-making world in Ireland changed radically in 1957 with the entry of Boland's, the bakers, into the biscuit market. Boland's was an old-established milling firm based at Grand Canal Quay, Dublin. Like Jacob's they had also been taken over in the 1916 Rising, where the rebels were under the command of Éamon de Valera.

Boland's were not entirely new to biscuit-making. The firm was set up as a bakery in Dublin around 1830. In 1870, Patrick Boland built a large bakery and shop in Capel Street, which became the headquarters of the firm. Quakers enter the picture here too, when, in 1873, Patrick Boland purchased the mill of Messrs Pim at Grand Canal Quay to ensure a supply of flour to the bakery. At the time of purchase, there were twenty-three pairs of stones grinding corn into flour. Boland added eighteen more and, in 1880, replaced twenty-three of these with a new roller system invented by an American, J. H. Carter. Boland's was the first mill in these islands to use this revolutionary new method of milling. In 1874, Boland erected the City of Dublin Bakery in nearby Ringsend Road where bread was baked on an extensive scale.

By the time the Capel Street premises were extended in 1888, they included a biscuit-making department. Boland expanded into the prosperous suburb of Kingstown (Dún Laoghaire) and opened Boland's Model Bakery there. He also had two retail shops in the township, one at 9 George's Street and the other at 14 Cumberland Street. Fifty-three workers were employed in the bakery in Kingstown and every morning before six o'clock, twenty-five horses and vans left the bakery with bread for the surrounding area. At the end of the nineteenth century, Boland's employed some eight hundred people in total.

Competition is no bad thing, and the arrival of Boland's in the biscuit market forced many changes on Jacob's. Also in 1957, Jacob's in Dublin attempted to buy back the export trade from Liverpool, but could not afford it as a result of the government restrictions on profit. This, together

Bolands, Capel Street Dublin in 1888.

with the arrival of Boland's, forced Jacob's to look anew at its vital home market. Despite difficult economic conditions, Jacob's had managed to innovate and develop in the restricted market in which it found itself. However, there was a natural tendency to rest on its laurels in the absence of competition in the Republic of Ireland. A measure of complacency, and the fact that the firm was in the hands of close-knit families for so long, resulted in a certain amount of paternalism and conservatism. An example of the thinking in the company was evident in the practice of the commercial travellers who arrived in their various destinations around Ireland, booked into their hotels and waited for the customers to come to them! It was clear that major changes were needed to respond to the challenge from Boland's.

In 1959, J. P. Fox retired, Edward C. Bewley, became chairman, and Gordon Lambert became marketing manager, with, as he remarks 'responsibility for keeping our competitor, Boland's, at bay'. As was said at his retirement celebration, Fox, for thirty years, 'was the factory'. He was remembered for the introduction of air-conditioning into the factory, an early form of air-tight packaging, and sloping ovens, noted in the last chapter. Bewley was a grandson of William Bewley who had joined the firm in 1863, and followed his father's footsteps into Jacob's. He held an

Bertie Ahern, T.D., then Minister for Finance, samples a biscuit presented to him by Leo O'Donnell, Managing Director.

MA degree from Cambridge and became a chartered accountant in Dublin. His brother William also entered the firm. Gordon Lambert had joined the firm in 1944. His family were well-known in the veterinary and sporting world in Dublin. His father and grandfather were veterinary surgeons based in a large practice in Richmond Street. His father was the well-known cricketer, R.H. Lambert, known as 'the W. G. Grace of Ireland'. The business background was on his mother's side of the family. His mother's family were the owners of Mitchell's of Grafton Street, the well-known confectioners and restaurateurs. He was educated at Sandford Park School, Ranelagh, Rossall School, Lancashire and Trinity College, Dublin, where he graduated with BA and B. Comm. degrees. He was also appointed to the board of the company in 1959.

These changes in Jacob's coincided with economic recovery in Ireland after the stagnation of most of the 1950s, and the appointment of Seán Lemass as Taoiseach in 1957. In many ways, the career of Gordon Lambert shadowed that of Lemass on the larger national canvas, indeed one ex-employee dubbed Lambert 'the Lemass of Jacob's'. Seán Lemass was aware of Lambert's talents; when he was appointed a member of the Electricity Supply Board, a letter of congratulations from Lemass spoke of his 'intelligence, energy and dedication'. In 1958, T. K. Whitaker's five-

The allure and excitement of the Race Track were evoked in Ascot Cream.

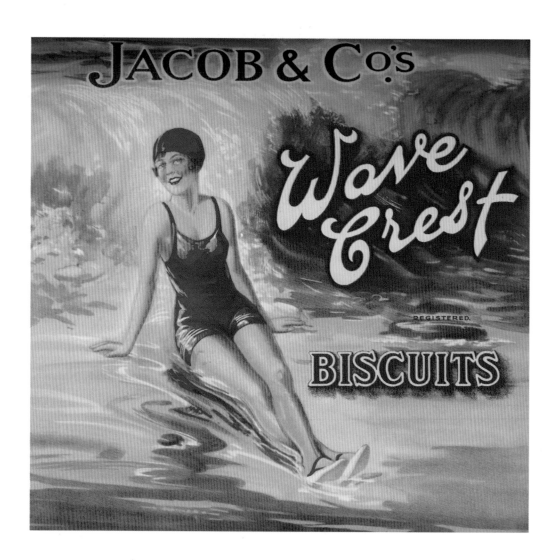

Wave Crest, a forerunner of the Cream Cracker, was a Jacob's original from the 1880s.

Popular packets from the 1980s.

Irish Biscuits' display at a recent food fair.

year plan for economic expansion was introduced, and between 1959 and 1968, industrial output in the Republic of Ireland rose by 82%.

Paralleling this, a revolution in retailing and merchandising was also beginning. The arrival of supermarkets sounded the death-knell for biscuit tins. Air-tight packets, an innovation introduced by Jacob's in 1927, now came into their own. As well as being welcomed by the consumer, the new packaging helped improve bulk handling methods. Loose biscuits in tins were still sold to hotels and caterers. The new packets also benefited from the introduction of five-colour photogravure printing. Airtights proved so popular that in 1959 the firm was working overtime two days a week to meet demand. In anticipation of the move to air-tights, a new logo, the Jacob's striking red flash, was devised and introduced in 1958. This replaced the well-known 'Trumpeter' logo which was in use since the 1930s. The distinctive new symbol became familiar to shoppers all over Ireland, so intensifying the company's image. At the other end of the production process, the bulk handling of ingredients such as sugar and flour, was brought in.

A singular success had been achieved in 1960 when Cream Crackers were allowed into the United States under their own name; they had been barred until then because they had no cream in them.

The company underwent many technical and structural changes. A big step forward in computerisation took place in February 1964 when a new ICT computer arrived in Bishop Street – it cost £65,000 and was delivered in ten crates and weighed almost four tons! Area sales managers were appointed and sales and marketing were backed up by changes in merchandising and advertising. More resources were put into advertising and clever public relations work.

It was felt, however, that much work still needed to be done. The export market was still seen as disappointing; in 1962 it amounted to only £176,000. Increased efforts were made to penetrate the United States market. The Irishness of the product was stressed; in 1963 a round tin featuring sketches of scenes from the songs of Percy French, such as The Mountains of Mourne and Phil the Fluther was being exported. Other tins featured well-known Irish beauty spots. The Irish Tourist Board wrote to Jacob's to inform them that they had received a letter from two ladies in California stating that they had seen an Irish lakeside view on a Jacob's biscuit tin and they wished to rent a cottage near it!

Hopes were high that greater profits could still be achieved in the expansion of the home biscuit business. The Chairman pointed out in 1959 that the per capita consumption of biscuits in Britain was twice that of Ireland, but that the gap was narrowing as a result of acting on the findings of market surveys and the introduction of advanced marketing techniques, increased public relations, and new packaging.

Augmenting advertising and merchandising, public relations were developed by the increasingly popular visit to Jacob's factory. In the late 1950s, some 10,000 visitors were welcomed onto the factory floor every year. One visitor, James Scannell, remembers a visit in 1968, which his mother arranged for himself and a school friend. They started off with the Cream Cracker line, where, James recalls, 'we were supplied with paper bags and permitted to help ourselves from the production lines, and we came away with three-quarter pound of extremely fresh biscuits which crumbled on touch'. At the end of the visit each visitor was presented with a small tin containing a selection of Jacob's biscuits. James' tin was about the size of a school mathematic's set box; he observes: 'mine has survived down through the years, having been used as late as 1993 as a pen case for use at a professional examination'.

In the early 1960s, Jacob's had the inspired idea of associating themselves with the glamorous world of aviation then opening up to the general public in Ireland. In January 1961, Jacob's sponsored the Radió Éireann programme 'Come Fly With Me', with Harry Thuillier. The programme literally took to the air and interviewed people on Aer Lingus planes all round the world, visits to such glamorous places as New York being particularly popular. In September 1961, Jacob's chartered a plane to fly the first commercial flight from the new Cork airport with a group of its competition-winners on board. The winners had succeeded in placing the six best-selling Jacob's biscuits in the correct order. Among the personalities to greet the lucky travellers were Tony O'Reilly, the businessman, and Christy Ring, the famous hurler. It was pointed out on the occasion that the biscuit firm had played a small but important part in the flight of the first Aer Lingus plane, *Iolar*, in May, 1936 – the spare parts were carried in a Jacob's biscuit tin!

In October 1961, Frankie Byrne was appointed Public Relations Officer. Frankie was from Dublin and had gone to school in the Loreto Abbey. Her father was a sporting journalist with the *Irish Press*. She had worked for eleven years as secretary to the Brazilian Consulate in Dublin, and had been appointed honorary consul. She worked for a short period as a researcher in Radió Éireann. She had been with McConnell's advertising and eventually opened her own public relations' agency.

In 1963, Frankie Byrne began the radio programme for which she

Frankie Byrne who, through the radio programme Women's Page, became the voice of Jacob's.

became a household name in Ireland. 'Women's Page', from the people 'who make better biscuits better every day' in the words of the famous catchphrase, went out on Radió Éireann every Tuesday at 1p.m. Frankie became Ireland's first well-known agony aunt by accident. She used to read out selections from the women's pages of magazines, but when a strike broke out among journalists, her material dried up. She had begun to receive letters from listeners, which she read out. They soon began to pour in and the programme became extremely popular. Frankie is also remembered for her devotion to Frank Sinatra, and only played his records on the show.

Most of the letters were quite innocent by today's standards, usually from young women suffering from shyness, especially as regards the opposite sex. Many asked advice on their boyfriends and whether she thought their intentions were serious or not. Letters were also received from young, and not so young, men. While she took the letters seriously, answering some privately and referring some to experts, she recognised a joke when she saw one. She easily identified fake letters and took great pleasure in exposing them as such. She held the opinion that the fact that she was not married herself gave her an objective view on marital diffi-culties. Her experience with the problems of courting couples gave her a strong belief in the need for pre-marriage courses, an idea taken up by the clergy and others.

The *annus mirabilis* of 1961 for Jacob's was rounded off with another brilliant coup. With the advent of Telefís Éireann, the Irish national television service, Jacob's conceived the idea of instituting annual broadcasting awards recognising the outstanding achievements of broadcasters, writers, technicians, and production personnel. Together with Frankie Byrne, who worked closely with Radió Telefís Éireann, the idea was brought to fruition. The first Jacob's television awards were presented by the then Taoiseach, Seán Lemass, in the Bishop Street factory in 1961. In 1969, the awards were extended to include radio. The award winners were chosen by a panel of radio and television critics in the national press. Many of the staff of Bishop Street became involved in the awards ceremony. The factory was turned into a veritable night club for the occasion, and a hundred employees were on duty as hosts

The actor, Hilton Edwards, is presented with a Jacob's Radio and Television Award by Gordon Lambert in 1965.

for the visiting celebrities and their guests. After ten years, in 1972, as Jacob's began the transition to Tallaght, the awards ceremony was moved to various venues in the provinces.

During this period, the awards were presented in Cork, Galway, Waterford, Wexford and Limerick. In 1977, the ceremony returned to Bishop Street, shortly before the old premises were finally vacated. Later venues included the National Film Studios of Ireland, Ardmore, Co. Wicklow, Leopardstown Race Club, Co. Dublin and other Dublin venues such as the the premises of the Royal Dublin Society and the Burlington and Jury's hotels. The winners made up a galaxy of Irish television and radio stars. A special 20th year award was presented to Gay Byrne in 1982.

In appreciation of Jacob's 21 years' support of RTÉ, in 1987, RTÉ made the unprecedented gesture of presenting the chairman of Jacob's, Gordon Lambert, with a bronze replica of the sculpture by Michael Warren situated outside the Radio Centre in Donnybrook. The presentation was made by the then Chairman of RTÉ, Fred O'Donovan.

A revolution in advertising also took place at this time. Advertising up to this had been occasional and haphazard and the budget ran to only a tiny fraction of Jacob's turnover. In conjunction with McConnell's and Royd's advertising agencies, individual brand advertising was introduced, starting with Cream Crackers and then moving on to Fig Rolls, increasing the budget to 5% of turnover. In 1962, Jacob's placed the first full-colour advertisements ever to appear in the *Irish Times*.

The spectacular Fig Roll campaign is still remembered by many Irish people. This began as a newspaper campaign seeking the whereabouts of a certain Jim Figgerty. Many mistook the notices as genuinely seeking a missing person and they created a huge public response. It turned out however that Jacob's sought Figgerty because he was the only person who knew how to get the figs in the Fig Rolls. The campaign went from strength to strength and the actor, Paddy Griffin, became known the length and breadth of Ireland when he played Figgerty in television advertisements. Another phase of the campaign spawned such catch-phrases as 'Who cares, Habibi, they're gorgeous', in reply to the question 'How do Jacob's get the figs into the Fig Rolls?'.

In 1962, during the Dublin Theatre Festival, a window dressing competion was organised by Jacob's to coincide with the introduction of their new Fair City tin of biscuits. Also in that year a new Town Office, where small Dublin retailers came to collect biscuits, was opened at Peter's Row. A quarter of a million tins of biscuits per year were handled over the counter in the office. All of the publicity and advertising were paying off, and, in 1962, the company recorded the biggest sales in its history, with turnover increasing by 10% between 1961 and 1963.

Attempts at diversification were a feature of these buoyant years. 'Maisies', an expanded corn snack food, was produced in 1959. Ready-made soup was tried as moulds used to make chocolate bars were found to be suitable for making solid soup which was liquified in the home. However, the soup, made on behalf of the Quorn company, was only a short time on the market when the more convenient packet soups arrived and put an end to the Jacob's product. Maisies and Quorn soup were discontinued in 1961.

In August 1963, the Gye Cracker was presented to the public. The idea was a brilliant one; as E. C. Bewley told the assembled invitees at the launch, it was the result of a marriage of the 'wealthy Guinness to the poor Jacob's girl.' After two years of experimentation, Jacob's obtained exclusive rights to use Guinness yeast extract, an integral component of the famous black stout, as the main ingredient in a savoury biscuit. Market research had shown an increased interest in savoury biscuits, and the product obtained the full support of the Guinness board. Therefore, the famous Guinness smell that has hung over St. James' Gate for centuries joined the sweet smell of freshly-baked biscuits that clung around Bishop Street. Despite claims that the new cracker was waterproof and would not get soggy, no matter what was spread on it, sales were disappointing and it was soon withdrawn. Problems had also arisen in the working relationship between Jacob's and Guinness's – the marriage ended in divorce! A decade later, negotiations were entered into with Nabisco in the United States, and the distribution of the highly successful Ritz Crackers was obtained.

This period also saw huge changes to the physical structure of the factory. Early in 1964, demolition got under way for the implementation of modernisation plans. Many of the old buildings were knocked down to make way for a more co-ordinated and automated production flow, and a new hangar-type warehouse for storage. Increased automation led to a reduction in the workforce, especially women. In these years, the numbers were cut by 600 to a total of 900 women and 500 men. Male losses were mainly in departments such as joinery and metalwork, not directly connected with biscuits. The small home market and limited export possibilities because of the Liverpool firm's exclusive interests, together with the 'familiar Irish problem' of much variety in small quantities, were also cited for the losses. Trying to produce a large variety of biscuits for a limited market meant small and inefficient runs. A biscuit like Cream

Cracker could be baked all day, every day. On the other hand, however, in the case of a biscuit like Celtic Shortbread, sufficient could be baked in one shift to do for a few months, but they would not keep, so they had to be baked in even shorter shifts. Cream Crackers were still the biggest seller, and another 60 varieties were sold separately and 40 more in assorted collections. A change in taste was noted, with an increase in the sale of chocolate biscuits. This was regarded as healthy for profits because turnover in relation to the weight was much higher.

Another innovation took place in relation to fuel. In 1959, a boiler was converted to burn turf. It consumed fifteen tons of turf a day and turned out to be so efficient that it was decided to switch the other two to the native Irish fuel, and scrap the old one which had outlived its usefulness. The company estimated that the change would reduce the fuel bill by 30% and commented that the switch was made because the price of turf was stable and so it would not be at the mercy of foreign vagaries. Also the annual fuel bill of £25,000 would be a great help to the Irish economy. In 1962, as the price of oil began to rise, it was decided to turn to the exclusive use of turf.

A review of the state of the company at the beginning of 1964 reiterated some old problems. It was pointed out that some biscuits had a higher labour intensity than others; assortments, for instance, had to be packed by hand and could cause problems with recruitment when demand was high coming up to Christmas. There were dispatch problems, as each traditional tin had to be weighed and billed for accordingly. Packets now accounted for 65% of total output. Jacob's had 80% of the Irish biscuit market, but falling tarrifs on imported goods, including biscuits, partly as a result of the Anglo-Irish Free Trade Agreement, began to increase competition. Ireland was regarded as more biscuit-conscious than the continent but less so than Britain. It was admitted that the arrival of Boland's biscuits had given Jacob's a new competitive spirit, but that there was still immense goodwill towards Jacob's in Ireland.

Increased competition from at home and abroad took its toll. In September 1961, it was announced that the Derry biscuit department of Brewster and Co. was to close with the loss of sixty-two jobs. The company had been making biscuits for seventy-five years and they were sold throughout Northern Ireland and Co. Donegal. The company stated that its biscuit-making operation was no longer economic. Shortly afterwards, Jacob's signalled confidence in the future. It was stated that the company had adapted to the new self-service conditions in which the customer was directly selecting goods, as opposed to the shopkeeper doing it for him or her. The challenge of possible entry into the Common Market was being met by a twenty-year plan in which the priority would be to make the company more competitive.

Greater productivity and efficiency paid off with increased profits in the 1960s. The decade started with a net profit before taxation in 1960 of £284,108 compared to £189,404 the previous year. In 1962, twenty-five million more Cream Crackers were sold than in the previous year, partly due to new packaging. However, all this was not achieved without tensions, for instance, in July of 1961, there was a lightning strike in the Bakehouse. Work stopped shortly after 8.a.m., but was resumed at noon.

An interesting order was obtained in the mid-sixties which was indicative of the Cold War conditions then prevailing. The Department of Defense ordered a consignment of special cracker-type biscuits which were to be stored in case of nuclear attack. The order took three months to complete and the biscuits were sealed in special skips and sent to the Curragh Camp, where, for all we know, they still remain!

The years following the entry of Boland's into the biscuit market were the most exciting and buoyant the company had ever experienced. A strong media and public relations exposure, and a greatly enhanced corporate image, resulted in the highest sales in the history of the company, and saw Jacob's emerge as a leader on the Irish industrial scene. No-one foresaw that within a few short years, the company would merge with its greatest rival, make a painful move from its traditional home, and almost face extinction.

CHAPTER FIVE

On the Move – A New Home in Tallaght

With the signing of the Anglo-Irish Free Trade Agreement in 1965 together with the possibility of entry into the Common Market on the horizon, the boards of Jacob's and Boland's began to look at the idea of a merger. The complex story of mergers and amalgamations in the biscuit industry began in 1921 in Britain when Huntley and Palmer and Peek, Frean merged to form Associated Biscuit Manufacturers Limited. Huntley and Palmer have been noted already; Peek, Frean originated in 1887 when one Mr Peek, a London tea merchant, founded a biscuit-making business for his two sons. The sons had no interest in the concern and left the business, and their place was taken by their cousin, George Frean. In 1960, W. & R. Jacob & Company (Liverpool) Ltd. merged with Associated Biscuits.

Jacob's in Dublin were already spreading their wings, and bought a controlling stake in Smith's Potato Crisps (Ireland). The UK Smith's group maintained a minority stake in the Irish Smith's and agreed to provide the necessary technical assistance for the production of crisps of the highest quality. The Irish crisp market was a highly competitive one, the top brand by far and away being Tayto, in which the US group Beatrice Foods had a controlling interest. Some years previous to this, a serious challenge had come from Mr Perri crisps, but the arrival of Smith's on the Irish scene had not been successful to that point and the company had lost substantial sums. Prior to the involvement by Jacob's, Smith's and Tayto had been in discussions but these proved fruitless. Jacob's faced an uphill battle to shake the grip of the popular Tayto crisps in Ireland.

FORMATION OF IRISH BISCUITS
In many ways the move to merge with Boland's was a pre-emptive strike by Jacob's. They feared that an outside interest might make an attempt to take over Boland's with its sizeable productive capacity. In particular, in 1965 there was much talk of Garfield Weston being interested, if only as a supplier to his rapidly-expanding Power Supermarket chain in Ireland, but nothing came of this. On the export side, Boland's had done well, gaining substantial business from Marks & Spencer in Britain, for whom they made Cream Crackers worth £150,000 per annum under the 'St. Michael' name. They also exported one and a half million Cream Crackers per annum to thirty-three centres in such places as Iceland, Italy,

Bermuda, Beirut, Holland and Hong Kong. A number of large contracts in Canada were of particular importance. This impressive export record, which was created in less than a decade, contrasted with Jacob's and indicated how many potential exports were lost as a result of the restrictive arrangements with the English company.

The Jacob's/Boland's merger was in line with the policy of the Committee on Industrial Organisation, which was investigating the state of Irish industry with entry to the European Economic Community looming. With the arrival of Boland's, the market, which was still very much tariff-protected, expanded. Between 1959 and 1966, Jacob's sales increased by 90%. At the time of the merger, Jacob's had 80% of the market, Boland's about 15% and foreign biscuits 5%. Jacob's were selling 18,000 tons of biscuits a year and Boland's 3,000.

Both companies realised that international competition could be best faced by pooling resources. A new company was incorporated in 1966 under the name Irish Biscuits Limited. This company manufactured and marketed biscuits under the brand names Jacob's and Boland's. The right to the Jacob's name abroad remained with the English company. All the Directors of Jacob's became Directors of Irish Biscuits with Edward C. Bewley as Chairman. In order to represent the Boland's interest, Kevin A. Mulcahy was co-opted to the board of Jacob's and Patrick J. Murphy co-opted to the board of Irish Biscuits: both were Boland's Directors, and the Boland's Deansgrange factory remained in production. The Boland's milling operation remained separate and Jacob's agreed to continue to obtain part of its flour requirement from it. The new venture required careful planning of its marketing strategy so as not to affect the level of turnover achieved by each company up to the time of the merger.

DECISION TO MOVE TO TALLAGHT
Two years after the formation of Irish Biscuits, the concentration of production on one site was planned. Major problems continued with the

Boland's premises in Deansgrange, Co. Dublin at the time of the merger with Jacob's in 1966.

Bishop Street plant, owing to the cramped conditions and growing traffic congestion. In 1968, PA Management Consultants were brought in to study, in conjunction with the company, the options open to it. These were identified as (a) modernising Bishop Street; (b) moving to Deansgrange; and (c) building a new factory on a green field site. Much discussion ensued and intense research was carried out, with thirty major biscuit factories around the world visited. Eventually the decision was taken to purchase a 40-acre green field site on the outskirts of Dublin at Tallaght, and move all production there. The amalgamation of the Deansgrange factory with the main production plant was a logical move after Boland's and Jacob's merged, and a move from Bishop Street was becoming imperative. Many city companies were moving to green field sites due to production congestion and transport difficulties. The Bishop Street premises had grown piecemeal, and had become an engineer's nightmare. It's eighteen acres had swallowed a coach-building firm, a chapel, a graveyard, two public houses, a foundry and a dispensary. There were conveyor belts everywhere, and its five floors and twenty-four lifts made continued operation there very difficult.

A major factor in the decision to re-locate was that many Jacob's workers had already moved from the city centre. A high proportion of them now came from an area extending well into the south side of Dublin. About 60% of the Jacob's workforce lived in the Crumlin and Walkinstown areas, adjacent to Tallaght, having moved there from the Liberties and the environs of Bishop Street as a result of the erection of housing schemes by Dublin Corporation in the years before and after World War II. Others were now moving to the new satellite suburbs further south and west, and a good number of new mortgages were linked to Jacob's wage packets. Deansgrange would have posed a problem in that it was far from most of the Jacob's workforce, and had a limited potential as a supply of workers. On the other hand, the move to Tallaght did not suit many Boland's workers and a number of them gave up the job when the move was made.

The estimated cost of the move was £4.5 million, £2.9 million in respect of building works and £1.6 million for machinery and equipment. Finance was sought and building got under way at Belgard Road, Tallaght. An application was made to the Industrial Development Authority for a re-equipment grant towards the cost of the capital work involved in the re-location and the maximum grant of £350,000 was allocated.

Jeffrey B. Jenkins, then Deputy Chairman, pointed out an interesting example of historical continuity. In 1885 the reel ovens to make the first

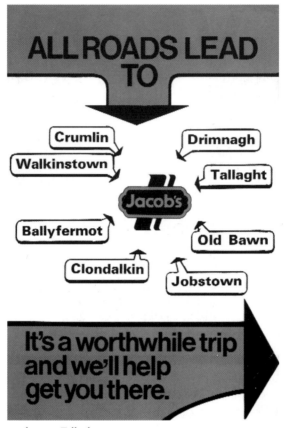

Leaflet enticing workers to Tallaght.

Cream Crackers, supplied by Fowler and Rockwell of New York, were purchased by a loan arranged through the Royal Bank of Ireland from Brown, Shipley, merchant bankers. Almost one hundred years later, it was Brown, Shipley who handled the UK Board of Trade's overseas export credit guarantee for the UK goods and services for the Tallaght project.

No sooner had work begun at Tallaght than things began to go awry. The logistics of moving two complex productive units to a green field site were underestimated. The construction and the perfection of the heating in the new high-tech ovens, which were over a hundred yards in length, took up to a year, and there were long delays in delivery times of key equipment. Matters outside Irish Biscuit's control seemed to conspire against the company. From the time of the decision to move to Tallaght to the actual move, inflation went from single to double figures. Serious interruptions in supplies to customers as a result of an industrial dispute did not help. In early 1969, Deansgrange shut down for eight weeks and Bishop Street for four, so that for some weeks there was hardly a Boland's

Jacob's chairmen 1979–1999: C. Gordon Lambert 1979–1986 (top left), Leo O'Donnell 1986–1991 (top right) and M. Desmond McGuane 1991–1999 (centre).

or Jacob's biscuit in the shops, and their foreign competitors began to make inroads in their market.

In 1970, despite sales for the first time in the history of the company of over one million pounds, a prolonged bank strike and the collapse of Jacob's new computer system caused serious disruption. It took nine months to get the computer system back in operation. In the meantime, customers had to be visited to sort out their accounts. Maintaining working capital under the constraints of a limited bank balance became difficult and problems arose in managing stock levels.

FINANCIAL CRISIS

By 1971, the company was in serious trouble trying to maintain three operations at once, factories in Bishop Street and Deansgrange and a building site in Tallaght. An expert financial controller, Leo O'Donnell, a chartered accountant and later to become Managing Director, was recruited to assist. It was clear that a liquidity strain on funding such a

Silos

Social Club

Pump House

Storage Tanks

Credit Union

Main Entrance

Factory

Canteen

Offices

Warehouse

Garage

Aerial view of Irish Biscuits' Tallaght complex in 1999.

massive capital investment would require substantial outside borrowing. A financial package was negotiated from February to September 1971 and it took much ingenuity to steer the company through the liquidity crisis of these months. An eighty-page document was agreed between the company and a consortium of lenders, led by Allied Irish Investment Bank. The agreement entailed the appointment of external directors to the board of Jacob's to accommodate the financial interests. The Tallaght project was scaled back; expenditure on a warehouse and office block was put on hold. Another condition was the enfranchisement of the 'B' shares, which ended control by the Jacob and Bewley families; Jacob's now became a fully-fledged Irish public company unencumbered by family interests.

It had long been the practice of the Jacob family that the young members should spend a year 'at the ovens' before they went on to other positions in the firm, and numerous members held managerial positions in the firm up to recent times. The last person bearing the Jacob name to work in the company was Michael Jacob, son of A. Neil Jacob, who started as a trainee in 1963, but left after nine months to join the RAF.

Shortly after the financial package was agreed, phase one of the move to Tallaght including the re-location of the Deansgrange production was achieved. Phase two saw the completion of the move from Bishop Street and the centralising of all production in Tallaght.

While the lengthy financial negotiations were taking place, problems seemed to accumulate. In the middle of discussions with the lending institutions, a major strategical component of the completion of the Tallaght move came unstuck. This had envisaged substantial exports of the famous Jacob's mallow biscuits, Kimberley, Mikado and Coconut Creams, to England under the Irish Biscuits' label. Test marketing of such a product in Britain had been successful. The launch of the products in England in the second half of 1971 indeed proved very successful. However, in the aftermath of Bloody Sunday in Derry at the beginning of 1972, everything changed. There was a huge reaction against Irish goods in Britain, and the heavy Irish branding of the mallow biscuits was a victim of this. This resulted in what was known in the factory as 'the mallow mountain', which could not have happened at a worse time.

Despite the difficulties, the board seemed to be getting a grip on the situation, when, in 1973, the company was hit by a body blow – what has become known as 'The Great Russian Grain Robbery'. Russia, buying through agents in many parts of the world, collared the American wheat export allocation, unknown to the American government. This pushed up the price of the remaining wheat from £40 to £100 a ton overnight, with serious financial implications for Irish Biscuits.

An urgent request was made to the National Prices' Commission for an increase in prices, but a decision was delayed and submissions to the commission were cut by £300,000 in the latter part of 1972. Heavy trading losses began to accumulate. The energy crisis then hit and there was a shortage of some raw materials. The cost of raw materials available rose from £2.8 million in 1972 to £4.8 in 1973. Also the transfer from the two old factories to Tallaght saw the disappearance again of some Boland's and Jacob's lines from the shops. The government decision not to include biscuits, especially Cream Crackers, in its list of food necessities from which VAT was to be removed, dealt a temporary blow. A pretax profit of £60,000 was returned for 1973, representing a disastrous one per cent on capital. To put this in context, in the late 1960s profits had been around £500,000, but had fallen to £300,000 in 1971/72. Bank borrowings were up to £2 million despite the sale and leaseback of the old Bishop Street building.

END OF PRODUCTION AT DEANSGRANGE AND BISHOP STREET
Further property deals did ease the situation somewhat. Production at Deansgrange was finally wound down in August 1972 and the factory sold. The Deansgrange plant and property in Kevin Street realised £250,510. The controlling interest in Smith's Crisps was also sold to John Daly and Company in 1973.

A re-appraisal of the export situation was urgently required. It was decided that in the 1975-78 period, Irish Biscuits would concentrate on selling products under retailers' and other manufacturers' brand labels. This was not new to the company as Boland's had very successfully engaged in such a venture with the Marks & Spencer chain. This new strategy met with success, and Cream Crackers were supplied to Littlewoods and the Club Milk range to Nabisco in Australia.

The Tallaght plant was officially opened on 17 November, 1975 by the Minister for Industry and Commerce, Justin Keating. Gordon Lambert spoke of the 'sometimes traumatic' dislocation involved in the move to Tallaght and the difficult years that the company had faced as a result of a world commodity crisis, massive increases in the cost of flour and other raw materials, followed by the energy crisis. Bishop Street remained in operation until 1977, and the last biscuit was baked in the old factory in April of that year.

Changing images: Jacob's logos from the 1930s to the present day.

The vacated Jacob's Bishop Street factory after its destruction by fire in 1987.

The lack of adequate office facilities at Tallaght, as a result of the shelving of building plans, was solved in 1974 when system-built offices, vacated by the Irish Management Institute, were purchased and relocated in the new complex. In 1976, a warehouse was finally built.

The company now had two primary objectives: to achieve profitability which would not only satisfy shareholders, but pay off interest to the financial institutions and prove to them that Jacob's were on the road to profitability; the other was to develop the market and keep the company's share. In the loss-making years of the early 1970s, the Jacob's share of the Irish market fell from about 85% to 60%, losing out to cheap imports from Britain. However, the company continued to engage in strong marketing and expensive advertising, and this prevented more erosion of its market share. The quality of the product was maintained, and the temptation to produce cheaper biscuits to compete with cheap imports, resisted. Major price increases were eventually introduced and much hard work was put into improving its share of the home market.

Unfortunately, after the Bishop Street premises passed out of Jacob's hands, they were left to fall victim to neglect and vandalism. As a result, much of the factory was destroyed by fire on the night of 20 May 1987. The City of Dublin Vocational Education Committee, which had bought the premises for £1.25 million in 1982, finally opened their fine new college at the Peter's Row end in 1994. The granite arches of the old loading bays were incorporated into the new building. On Bishop Street, a stone lintel still retains the engraving 'Offices' from Jacob's days. The Bishop Street corner with Bride Street was acquired by the State and the new National Archives of Ireland sited there.

The Tallaght factory and ancillary buildings were, at the time of their erection, the second largest Irish industrial site after Ferenka in Limerick. They eventually covered over thirty acres. In total contrast to the Bishop Street factory, the new production building was on one floor level, greatly facilitating the handling of materials and services. The old system of hoisting bags and moving bogies was gone forever. The new layout ensured the rapid movement of goods from department to department with the least possible delay or congestion.

The production building covers over six acres and, when built, had the largest floor space in Ireland under one roof. The scale of the building, which is without any internal partitions, is impressive. It is 318 metres (1040 feet) in length, or one-fifth of a mile, and 66 metres (217 feet) wide. The production building has a unique metal ceiling above which services such as steam, electricity and compressed air can be distributed to the required part of the factory. Air is changed on the factory floor every thirty minutes. When eventually completed, the total cost of the building work was nearly fifteen million pounds.

Under EEC rules, Associated Biscuit Manufacturers (ABM), of which Jacob's, Liverpool were a part since 1960, could have sold biscuits in Ireland under the Jacob's name. However, friendly relations were maintained with the English company, and amicable *ad hoc* arrangements were made with it, usually on a year-to-year basis. In 1975 it was felt that the time had come to arrive at some permanent arrangement with the English company. The Dublin company negotiated exclusive rights to supply Northern Ireland with Jacob's biscuits, in return for the complete surrender of the Jacob's name overseas. The Northern Ireland market was worth almost one million pounds and guaranteed an extra fifty jobs in Dublin; the overseas turnover given up in exchange was reckoned at about £200,000. There was ample scope for expansion in Northern Ireland, as Jacob's had 20% of the market share there. The Northern Ireland market had already been growing and to service that, and in anticipation of expansion, a fourteen-acre site was bought near Hillsborough, Co. Down in 1967 and a depot built at a cost of £150,000 to replace the existing one in Belfast. The agreement also meant that the company's policy of producing own brand biscuits for United Kingdom companies could continue.

Jacob's Variety Group, winners of John Player Tops of the Town, 1982.

State intervention in the form of £523,639 in aid from Taiscí Stáit and £92,197 from Fóir Teoranta was designed to safeguard employment in the years that the company found itself on the knife-edge. Financial problems persisted however, and more capital was sought. In March 1976, £791,000 was raised from shareholders in a 1 for 3 rights issue which sold at 55p per share. Shares were also sold to Associated Biscuit Manufacturers. ABM had an 11.5% shareholding in Jacob's, Dublin since 1974 and this was increased to 21.21% in 1976. In 1978, the financial situation still did not look good; creditors were owed £4.6 million and there was cash in hand of only £25,000. The following year, the Irish Biscuit's management proposed to increase ABM's holding to 29.96%. Their argument was that, as ABM had become a huge international company, Irish Biscuits would gain through product exchange, sharing of technical expertise and research and development. Jacob's managers would have the opportunity of gaining experience in plants all around the world. At first, the Irish government minister responsible for monitoring such matters, Des O'Malley, opposed such a move, but in the end was powerless to do anything about it. The sale of the shares raised £297,000.

MORE DIVERSIFICATION
One of the great strengths of Jacob's was its marvellous distribution system, reaching every supermarket and grocery shop, big and small, in

Ireland. To capitalise on this, a new phase of diversification began in the 1980s. As biscuit consumption remained stagnant or even declined, it was seen that the company needed to widen the base of its business. In November 1980, Jacob's bought a one-third share of two Northern Ireland companies, John McWhirr Ltd. and Valley Packing Company. Trading under the Valley Gold brand name, they were importers of dried and canned food, cereals, fruit and juices. Jacob's had the right to buy up to 75% of the company between 1982 and 1985. The companies traded exclusively in Northern Ireland but Jacob's saw the potential of expansion south of the border.

The following year, Jacob's began to distribute coffee under the brand Jacob's (pronounced Yacob's) Instant Coffee. This was one of the leading brands of coffee in Germany. The German company had no connection with the Irish one, but the coincidence of the name, added to the fact that the Irish market for an instant coffee was beginning to develop, encouraged the relationship. While the greater use of the existing distribution network by adding coffee and other grocery products to biscuits seemed to make sense, such a move required careful planning and was fraught with dangers and difficulties. The grocery market was a tough one in which to introduce new products, with much advertising necessary, and low margins; Jacob's did not find the going easy.

Acquisitions continued with the take-over of the business of the United Yeast Company (Ireland) Limited in 1988 through a new company, Unifood. The following year, new ground was opened when a British company, the Golden Glow Nut Company, was acquired.

In all this diversification, the core business was by no means neglected. Proof of this was seen in 1989 with the launch of one of the most successful products in many years. This was the Chocolate Kimberley. Kimberley was always a best-seller, but new imaginative product development, together with clever new marketing, introduced one of the company's oldest and most famous biscuits to a whole new generation. William Beale Jacob would have been proud.

In 1982, Nabisco, the American multi-national, bought out Associated Biscuit Manufacturers, including its 29.6% share of Jacob's. In the meantime, from the time of the Jacob/Boland merger, events were taking place in Europe which would have a bearing on the future of biscuit making in Ireland. In 1966, the company that would later became known as Groupe Danone was taking shape. In that year, two separate glass manufacturers, Glaces de Boussois and Souchon-Neuvesel, merged in order to cope with the growing French demand for glassware. Boussois specialised in plate glass for cars and buildings, and Souchon-Neuvesel made bottles. Both were keen to exploit the rapidly-growing demand for containers. During the 1960s, bottle manufacturers experienced unprecedented demand, with production tripling during the decade. The new business, named Boussois Souchon-Neuvesel or BSN, became one of France's biggest glass makers.

In 1973, BSN mounted a reverse takeover of the Gervais Danone dairy group. In 1990, BSN Danone bought the European operations of the American food giant Nabisco, including its share in ABM and Jacob's. BSN Danone was now the third largest food company in Europe and was Europe's chief producer of biscuits and snack foods, owning forty biscuit factories. In 1991, BSN Danone made a bid for total control of Jacob's. Jacob's management was favourable to the move. Leo O'Donnell, the managing director, expressed the board's feeling at the time: 'our strategy has been to find a partner. Technology and research and development requirements are becoming immensely expensive. Our expansion in the domestic market will be greatly strengthened and we will be able to provide different products. Abroad we can work through a very comprehensive distribution network. BSN is very strong in Europe, where the future lies'.

The recommended cash offer was very enticing to Jacob's shareholders. When they had last traded, Jacob's shares were selling at £2.90; BSN Danone offered £5 per share, which valued Jacob's at £59 million. This was nearly twenty times Jacob's earnings in 1990 and more than double the net assets of the company, which stood at £24 million. In the words of one press comment at the time, Danone 'risked being bowled over by shareholders rushing to acccept', and the required 50% of shareholders acceptance was easily gained. There was regret at the passing of an independent Irish company of such a long pedigree. As Bill McConnell, then Financial Director who became Managing Director in 1994, expressed it: 'in an emotional sense we were all sad to see Jacob's taken over, but the reality is that that was the way the European market was heading.' Changes were taking place in the Liverpool company as well; it moved its head office for a time to the famous biscuit town of Reading before moving back again to Liverpool in 1998. Its name change was permanent however, becoming Jacob's Bakery.

The experience of Jacob's as part of what is now known as Groupe Danone has been seen as positive. The vast bulk of the profits of Jacob's have been ploughed back into the company. In the first three years of Danone ownership, £14 million were invested in the company. The last

Some work never changes – on the factory floor in 2001.

ten years have seen much rationalisation and the launch of new products, both at home and abroad.

Jacob's brands, market leaders for a century and a half, still attract strong loyalty among consumers. Jacob's Fig Rolls are still Ireland's largest-selling biscuit. Indeed, with Fig Rolls and the mallow range, Jacob's have close to 100% market share. In 2000, the Fig Roll bar was successfully launched and in the following year the Fig Roll snack pack was introduced.

Writing from the perspective of 2001, the 150th year of the company, it appears that there are more changes on the horizon for Jacob's. The company has undergone many transformations since William Jacob spied the old coachyard in Peter's Row, and through them all it has triumphed. There seems little doubt that the fancy luxuries that have graced tea-tables throughout the land for over a century and a half will continue to do so well into the new millennium.

Jacob's in Literature

Charles Jacob was remembered by one Dublin employee as a little man with a beard, wearing kneebritches 'like George Bernard Shaw'. The employee described the kneebritches as 'economical trousers', worn to save cloth in the old frugal, thrifty Quaker tradition.

Memories of Charles by the playwright, Hugh Leonard, in his autobiographical novel *Home Before Night* are in a similar vein. Leonard's father, Mr Keyes, worked as a gardener for Charles Jacob at his house, known as Enderley, in Dalkey, Co. Dublin. On Sunday mornings, his father washed the Daimler in which the Jacob family went to Meeting. Unusually for the early 1900s, it was driven by a chauffeuse, a Miss Grubb. Every Christmas morning, Mr Keyes was presented with a pound note, a tin of biscuits and tumbler of Irish whiskey by his employer. On one occasion, Mr Keyes pocketed a halfpenny change he had got after an errand for Mr Jacob, as he did not want to disturb him for such a trifling sum. Later that day, he was called before his employer who demanded his halfpenny, stating 'halfpennies make shillings, shillings make pounds, and that is why I am sitting where I am and you are standing where you are'. Perhaps we are not being too harsh by stating that that little epigram sums up Quaker economic philosophy very well.

This is not the only reference to the Jacob family and their business in literature. It would be surprising if the great Dublin writer, James Joyce, whose work evokes for all time life in Dublin at the turn of the last century, did not refer to Dublin's greatest food industry. A reference to the most famous of all Jacob's products is found in the collection of short stories, *Dubliners*. In the first story, 'The Sisters', a young boy, recognised as Joyce himself, visits the house of a dead priest:

> We crossed ourselves and came away. In the little room downstairs we found Eliza seated in his armchair in state. I groped my way towards my usual chair in the corner while Nannie went to the sideboard and brought out a decanter of sherry and some wineglasses. She set these on the table and invited us to take a little glass of wine. Then, at her sister's bidding, she filled out the sherry into the glasses and passed them to us. She pressed me to take some cream crackers also but I declined because I thought I would make too much noise eating them. She seemed to be somewhat disappointed at my refusal and went over quietly to the sofa where she sat down behind her sister. No one spoke: we all gazed at the empty fireplace.

Taking Cream Crackers with a drink such as sherry is a custom that was very common, and, indeed, has survived.

In *A Portrait of the Artist as a Young Man*, Stephen Dedalus, the young university student, frustrated in love and angry, feels himself mocked by distorted reflections of his lover. One such manifestation is a girl he had glanced at, attracted by her small ripe mouth as she passed out of Jacob's biscuit factory; she had cried to him over her shoulder, eliciting a strong emotional response:

> – Do you like what you seen of me, straight hair and curly eyebrows?

> And yet he felt that, however he might revile and mock her image, his anger was also a form of homage.

In the 'Cyclops' episode in *Ulysses*, Leopold Bloom calls into Barney Kiernan's pub on Little Britain Street, near Green Street Courthouse. Bloom displeases the Irish nationalist, The Citizen (and his mangey dog, Garryowen) because he points out that Christ, like Bloom himself, was a Jew. As Bloom departs, The Citizen grabs an old biscuit tin described as a 'silver casket, tastefully executed in the style of ancient Celtic ornament, a work which reflects every credit on the makers, Messrs Jacob *agus* Jacob'. The Citizen took up the tin and what happened next is described in the mock heroic language characteristic of the episode: 'Begob he drew his hand and made a swipe and let fly. Mercy of God the sun was in his eyes or he'd have left him for dead. Gob, he near sent it into the county Longford'.

List of Partners/Directors
of W & R Jacob & Co of Dublin
(dates where known)

William B Jacob	Partner & Chairman	1851–1883
	Chairman & Managing Director	1883–1902
Robert Jacob	Partner	1851–1861
W Frederick Bewley	Partner	1864–1883
	Managing Director	1883–1922
Francis Bewley	Secretary	–1896
George J Newsom	Partner	1878–1883
	Managing Director	1883–1897
George N Jacob	Partner	1878–1883
	Managing Director	1883–1931
	Chairman	1902–1931
	President	1931–1937
Charles E Jacob	Managing Director	1896–1923
	Chairman	1931–1937
	President	1937–1941
Albert E Jacob	Managing Director	1896–1928
George A Newsom	Secretary	1896–1903
	Director	1903–1933
Thomas W Bewley	Secretary	1903–1920
	Director	1920–1934
Louis Bewley	Director/Secretary	1920–1930
	Director	1930–1936
Cedric W Jacob	Director	–1937
Arthur F Bewley	Director	–1930
Capt A R O'Conor	Director	1921–1951
Edward C Bewley	Secretary	1930–1937
	Director	1937–1959
	Managing Director/Chairman	1959–1971
	Chairman	1959–1975
	Director	1975–1978
John P Fox	Director	1931–1937
	Managing Director	1937–1959
	Director	1959–1965
Harold L Jacob	Chairman	1937–1949
William F Bewley	Secretary	1937–1947
	Secretary & Director	1947–1971
	Director	1971–1977

W Denis Hunton	Director	1940–1965
Roderic A O'Connor	Director	1943–1970
A Maitland Jacob	Chairman	1949–1959
Jeffery B Jenkins	Director	1947–1959
	Managing Director	1959–1971
	Deputy Chairman	1959–1975
	Chairman	1976–1979
	Director	1979–1982
A Neil Jacob	Director	1949–1972
Henry E Guinness	Director	1957–1968
C Gordon Lambert	Director	1959–1971
	Managing Director	1971–1979
	Chairman	1979–1986
	Director	1986–1987
Brian A Cox	Director	1966–1972
Alan H King	Director	1966–1970
Brian S Pim	Director	1966–1970
Kevin A Mulcahy	Director	1967–1985
Noel Griffin	Director	1970–1980
Eric S Cooke	Director	1970–1972
Leo O'Donnell	Director	1971–1979
	Managing Director	1979–1994
	Chairman	1991–1999
M Desmond McGuane	Director	1971–1992
	Chairman	1986–1991
Joseph B Gilroy	Director	1971–1972
Benjamin Power	Secretary	1971–1985
	Director & Secretary	1985–1992
Seamus P McGiolla Riogh	Director	1974–1991
Michael J Murphy	Director	1974–1991
M Gerard Murray	Director	1975–1977
W Gordon Medd	Director	1976–1985
William J McConnell	Director	1977–1992
	Secretary & Director	1992–1993
	Managing Director	1994–1999
Christopher B Barber	Director	1981–1982
Richard J Palmer	Director	1982–1983
Hugh Brown	Director	1983
D Royston Webb	Director	1983–1985
Jonathan R E Bewley	Director	1985–1998

Alistair C Mitchell-Innes	Director	1985–1988
Robert H Alcock	Director	1986–1989
Alan Reeve	Director	1988–1989
Philippe Jaeckin	Director	1989–2000
Christian Laubie	Director	1990–1995
Neil Murphy	Director	1998–2000
Thomas A. Hope	Director	1999–
Neil P. Saunderson	Director	2000–

Short Bibliography

The major sources for the history of Jacob's are the original documents including ledgers, notebooks, correspondence, catalogues, advertising material and newspaper cuttings held in the Jacob's Archive in Belgard Road, Tallaght. The following books have also been found useful.

L. M. Cullen, *An Economic History of Ireland Since 1660* [second edition] (London, 1987).

W. Hamish Fraser, *The Coming of The Mass Market* 1850–1914 (London, 1981).

Ormerod Greenwood, *The Quaker Tapestry* (London, 1990).

Henry W. Jacob, *A History of The Families of Jacob of Bridgewater, Tiverton and Southern Ireland* (private circulation, Taunton, 1929).

W. J. Jacob, 'The Dublin Family of Jacob', *Dublin Historical Record* vol. ii, Jun–Aug., 1940, pp 134–140.

Margaret Foster, *Rich Desserts and Captain's Thin: a Family and Their Times 1831–1931* (London, 1998).

T.A.B. Corley, *Quaker Enterprise in Biscuits: Huntley & Palmers of Reading, 1822–1972* (London, 1972).

J. J. Lee, *Ireland 1912–1985* (Cambridge, 1998).

Patricia McCaffrey, 'Jacob's Women Workers During the 1913 Lockout', *Saothar* 13.

Peter Murray, 'A Millitant Among the Magdalens? Mary Ellen Murphy's Incarceration in High Park Convent During The 1913 Lockout', *Saothar* 20.

Henry Parkinson and Peter Lund Simmonds (eds), *Dublin International Exhibition of 1865*, (London and Dublin 1866).

Ten Dublin Women (Women's commemoration and celebration committee, Dublin, 1991).

Maurice J. Wigham, *The Irish Quakers: A Short History of the Religious Society of Friends in Ireland* (Dublin, 1992).

Pádraig Yeates, *Lockout: Dublin 1913* (Dublin, 2000).

Index

Adelaide Hospital, 43
Aloysius, Fr., 46
Aer Lingus, 88
Ahern, Bertie, 86
Aigburth Ward, Liverpool, 30
Aintree, UK, 34, 40, 79, 83, 84
Allied Irish Investment Bank, 101
Anglo-Irish Free Trade Agreement, 93
Ardmore Studios, 91
Ashtown Tin Box Co., 62
Associated Biscuit Manufacturers Ltd., 95,
    105, 106, 107, 108
Association of Chambers of Commerce of
    the Irish Free State, 78
Astley, Philip, 22

Badcock, Mr, 30
Baker, George, 23
Baker & Co., 23
Ballybrack House, Killiney, 31
Bangor, Co. Down, 73
Barclays Bank, 2
Barmack's, 42
Barney Kiernan's pub, 111
Barrington's biscuit makers, 15
Baynard Press, 63
Beard, Freda, 63
Beatrice Foods, 95
Beckett, W. F., 27
Beirut, Lebanon, 96
Belfast, Co. Antrim, 66
Bell, George, 76
Béranger, Gabriel, 22
Berlin, Germany, 30
Bermuda, 96
Berwick Home, Rathfarnham, 75
Bewley, Edward C., 35, 54, 85, 96
Bewley, W. F., 28, 77
Bewley, William, 85
Bewley family, 2
Birkenhead, 65
Birmingham, UK, 79, 83
Bloody Sunday, 101
Boer War, 55

Boland, Patrick, 84
Boland's, 49, 61, 84, 85, 96
Bolger, Edward, 68
Boston, USA, 83
Brazilian Consulate, 88
Brewster & Co., 93
Bristol, UK, 83
British & Irish Steam Packet Co., 78
Broadstone Railway Station, 62
Broadway, USA, 48
Brown, Shipley, 98
BSN Danone, 108
Buncrana, Co. Donegal, 99
Burlington Hotel, 91
Byrne, Frankie, 88, 89

Cadbury's, 2, 30, 52, 54
California, USA, 87
Cambridge, 85
Canada, 50
Cardiff, Wales, 83
Carr's (of Carlisle), 27
Carter, J. H., 84
Ceylon, 50
Chicago, USA, 83
Children's Act (1908), 38
City of Dublin Bakery, 84
City of Dublin Vocational Education
    Committee, 104
Clarks' shoes, 2
Colbert, Con, 41, 45
Cold War, 94
Collins, Rita, 68
Commer van (for deliveries), 59
Committee on Industrial Organisation, 96
'Conche', 52
Connolly, James, 36, 40
Cope, George, 73
Cork, 3, 23, 88, 91
    French Street, 23
Cornwall, UK, 3
Cresca Company, 83
Crystal Palace, 1
Curragh Camp, 94

Cushen, Peter, 45, 46, 48
Cyprus, 50

Daily Mirror, 73
Daly, John, 102
Dargan, William, 19
Dawson, Mr, 41
Deansgrange, Co. Dublin, 97, 102
De Blacquer, Marie Emanuelle, 22
Dedalus, Stephen, 111
Dent, Dan, 70
Derry, 93, 101
Devon, UK, 3
Donegal, Co., 93, 99
Dorset, UK, 3
Doyle, John, 66
Doyle, Tom, 45, 48
Du Bedat, Jean, 22
Dublin
   Aungier Street, 22, 36, 40, 41, 76
   Ballsbridge, 30
   Belgard Road, 97
   Bishop Street, 22, 24, 25, 27, 30, 34,
      40, 41, 49, 51, 52, 54, 61, 62, 66,
      75, 79, 82, 87, 97, 98, 99, 102, 104,
      105
   Blackrock, 31
   Bride Street, 22, 75, 76
   Camden Street, 41
   Capel Street, 84
   Castleknock, 62
   Church Street, 46
   Churchtown, 62
   Clarendon Street, 27
   Coolock, 54
   Coombe, The, 25
   Crumlin, 97
   Dalkey, 110
   Digges Street, 48
   Drumcondra, 38
   Fairview, 38
   George's Street, 37
   Grand Canal Quay, 84
   Harold's Cross, 22
   Herbert Park, 30
   Inchicore, 62
   Kevin Street, 102
   Killiney, 31
   Leeson Street, 78
   Lower Kevin Street, 76
   New Row, 39, 42, 65
   New Street, 66
   North Wall, 36, 62
   Peter's Row, 1, 22, 23, 24, 25, 27, 48,
      67, 91, 104, 109
   Peter Street, 22, 25, 45, 48, 67
   Rathfarnham, 78
   Rathmines, 41
   Redmond's Hill, 43
   Richmond Street, 86
   Ringsend Road, 84
   Rutland Avenue, Crumlin, 73
   St. Stephen's Green, 39, 78
   Tallaght, 49, 54, 95, 96, 97, 100, 101,
      102
   Walkinstown, 97
   Wexford Street, 43
Dublin Chamber of Commerce, 78
Dublin Civic Museum, 72
Dublin Corporation, 97
Dublin International Exhibition (1907),
   30, 47
Dublin Metropolitan Police, 42
Dublin Port & Docks Board, 78
Dublin Theatre festival, 91
Duignan, Mary, 76
Dunlop, John Boyd, 62
Dunlop Tyre Factory, 62

Edwards, Hilton, 90
Electricity Supply Board, 86
Empress of Britain, 78
Enderley, Dalkey, 110
European Economic Community, 96, 105
   Common Market, 94
European Hotel, Dublin, 19

Farrington, Dr, 75
Federation of Chambers of Commerce of
   the British Empire, 78
Ferenka (of Limerick), 105
Fianna Fáil, 60
Figgerty, Jim, 91
Fitzgerald, Henry, 41, 43, 44
Florida, USA, 63
Fóir Teoranta, 106
Forsyth, Leslie, 72
Fowler & Rockwell, 98
Fox, George, 1–2, 3, 30
Fox, John P., 65, 67, 85
France, 50
Frederick, Leopold (Prince), 30
French, Percy, 87
'French Peter's', 22

Fry, Cyril, 62
Fry's, 2, 30, 52
Fry-Cadbury, 60

Galway, 73, 91
Gervais Danone, 108
Gilbert & Sullivan, 55
Gillespie, Sergeant, 75
Glaces de Boussois, 107
Golden Glow Nut Co., 107
Grace, W. G., 86
'Great Russian Grain Robbery', 101
Great Famine, 3
'Green, The', 22
Greece, 50
Griffin, Paddy, 91
Groupe Danone, 107–8
Grubb, Mary, 68
Grubb family, 2, 8
Guinness, 92
Guinness, Arthur, 29

Hackett, Rosie, 39
Hayes, James, 76
High Park Reformatory, 38
Hillsborough, Co. Down, 105
Holcombe, Alice, 3
Holland, 96
Hong Kong, 96
Howis, Henry, 2
Huguenots, 22
Huntley, Bourne & Steven's, 61, 62
Huntley, Joseph, 61
Huntley & Palmer, 2, 61, 95
Hunton, W. Denis, 34, 77

Iceland, 95
Industrial Development Authority, 97
Ingram, Captain, 24
Iolar, 88
Irish Biscuits Ltd., 96
Irish Free State, 77
Irish Jew, The, 48
Irish Management Institute, 104
Irish Press, 88
Irish Sugar Co., 50
Irish Times, 91
Irish Tourist Board, 87
Irish Transport & General Workers' Union, 35, 36, 38
Irish Women Workers' Union, 36, 39
Irish Worker, 35

Isle of Man, 73
Italy, 95

Jacob, A. Maitland, 34, 35, 77, 83
Jacob, A. Neill, 101
Jacob, Albert, 28, 31, 34, 77, 83
Jacob, Cedric, 34, 77, 83,
Jacob, Charles, 28, 29, 30, 31, 35, 77, 110
Jacob, George N., 28, 31, 35, 36, 38, 41, 77, 78
Jacob, Hannah, 31
Jacob, Henry William, 31
Jacob, Isaac, 3
Jacob, Joseph, 3
Jacob, Michael, 101
Jacob, Richard, 3
Jacob, Robert, 1, 3, 61
Jacob, W. Lansell, 35, 78
Jacob, William Beale, 1, 3, 23, 28, 31, 35, 78, 109
Jacob's Instant Coffee, 107
Jacob's Television & Radio Awards, 90
Jacob's Variety Group, 106
Jenkins, Dora, 78
Jenkins, Jeffrey B., 35, 97
Jenkins, Sir Walter, 78
Joyce, James, 110
    Dubliners, 110–11
    Portrait of the Artist as a Young Man, 111
    Ulysses, 111
Jury's Hotel, 91

Keating, Justin, 102
Keiley, Patrick, 8
Kelly, Bill, 45
Kelly, Luke, 50
Kenny's pub, 67
Keyes, Mr, 110
Killarney, Co. Kerry, 73
Kinahan & Co., Dublin, 17
King's (Liverpool) Regiment, 83
Kingstown, Co. Dublin (Dún Laoghaire), 40, 84

Lambert, Gordon, 80, 85–6, 90, 91, 93, 99, 102
Larkin, Delia, 36
Larkin, James, 35, 36, 38, 39
Lecky, W. E. H., 5
Le Fanu family, 22
Leinster Flour Mills, 49
Lemass, Seán, 86, 90

Leonard, Hugh, 110
  Home Before Night, 110
Leopardstown Race Club, 91
Leyland lorry (for deliveries), 40
Liberty Hall, 38
Limerick, 3
Littlewoods, 102
Liverpool, UK, 30, 34, 37, 39, 80, 81, 82,
  83, 84, 92, 73, 77, 79, 108
Liverpool Gas Company, 83
Lloyds Bank, 2
London depot, 83

McBride, Major John, 41
McCaffrey, Patricia, 34
McConnell's Advertising, 88, 91
McConnell, Bill, 108
McCormack, Elen, 76
McDonagh, Billy, 70
McDonagh, John, 48
McDonagh, Thomas, 41, 43
McEvoy, P., 45
McGuire, M. Desmond, 99
McWhirr, John, 107
Magdalen Asylum, Drumcondra, 38
Malahide Castle, 62
Malcolmson family, 2, 28
Mallin, Michael, 39
Manchester, UK, 30, 37, 39, 83
Marks & Spencer, 95, 102
Marsh & Co., 29
Mates, John, 76
Meath Hospital, 78
Minehead, UK, 3, 5
Mitchell's restaurant, 86
Molloy, Michael J., 48
Molyneux Chapel, Bride Street, 75
Molyneux House & family, 22
Molyneux Institute, 23
Monaghan, Fr., 46
Moon Bros., Birkenhead, 65
Morris, William, 65
Mount Jerome Cemetery, 22
Mountjoy Jail, 38
Mountrath, Co. Laois, 9
Mowatt, Henry P., 72
Mulcahy, Kevin A., 96
Murphy, Mary E., 37, 38
Murphy, P. J., 96

Naas, Co. Kildare, 49
Nabisco, 102, 108

National Archives of Ireland, 105
National Prices' Commission, 102
Newcastle, UK, 83
*New Commercial Directory for the Cities of
  Waterford and Kilkenny*, 13
Newsom, G. Arthur, 77
Newsom, G. J., 34
Newsom, Hanna H., 12
Newsom, John Charles, 23
Newsom, Samuel, 23
New York, USA, 83, 88, 48
New Zealand, 78
Norwich, UK, 83

O'Brien, Rose, 66
O'Connor, Lillie, 74
Odlum's, 49
O'Donnell, Leo, 99, 108
O'Donovan, Fred, 91
Old Dublin Society, 48
O'Malley, Des, 106
O'Malley, Dan, 47
Oregon, USA, 83
O'Reilly, Tony, 88
Orr, Thomas, 41, 44

PA Management Consultants, 97
Patricia chocolates, 60
Peek, Frean & Co., 7, 20, 95
Perry, biscuit makers, 20
Philippines, 54
Pim, Messrs, 84
Pim family, 2
Plymouth, UK, 83
Portarlington, Co. Laois, 49
Portland, USA, 83
Portlaw, Co. Waterford, 28
Portobello Barracks, 41
Portugal, 50
Powerscourt Arms Hotel, Enniskerry, 64
Powers-Samas system, 68
Power Supermarkets, 95
Price Waterhouse, 2
Purdy, W. J., 51

Quorn soup, 92

Radio Éireann, 48, 88
Rangoon, Burma, 56
Rathmines School, 78
Red Cross, 40
Registry of Deeds, Dublin, 17

Ring, Christy, 88
Rising (1916), 39, 40, 41–8.
Rossall School, Lancashire, 86
Rotunda Hospital, 78
Rowntree's, 2, 30, 52
Rowntree-Mackintosh, 60
Royal Bank of Ireland, 98
Royal College of Surgeons, 48
Royal Dublin Society, 91

St. Eustasia, Caribbean, 5
St. John's Ambulance Brigade, 75
St. Peter's churchyard, 37
Saint Mullins, Co. Carlow, 49
Sallins, Co. Kildare, 49
Sandford Park School, Ranelagh, 86
Scannell, James, 88
Shackleton's Mill, 36
Shaw, George Bernard, 110
Sherman, Mary (May), 69
Ship Street Barracks, 25
Sinatra, Frank, 89
Smith's Crisps, 95, 102
Social & Entertainment Committee, 73
Souchon-Neuvesel, 107, 108
South Africa, 56
Southampton, UK, 79, 83
Spain, 50
Sri Lanka, 54
Steenbock process, 56
Swan Hunter, 2
Swan Laundry, 67
Swanline Service, 67
Sweetman, Mary, 76
swimming pool (for employees), 71

Taiscí Stáit, 106

Tayto, 95
Temple Hill Cemetery, 31
Tennant & Ruttle, 59, 60
Thom's Directory, 20
Thuillier, Harry, 88
Tonge & Taggart, 22
Trafford Park, Manchester, 30
Trinity College, Dublin, 86
Trumpeter sign, 66, 87
Turkey, 50, 54
Unifood, 107
United Yeast Co., 107
Urney's, 54

Valley Gold, 107
Valley Packing Co., 107
Van Houten, Coenraad, 52
Vicars, Messrs T. & T., 13, 20

Walpole, Hanna Maria, 12
Walpole, James, 12, 21
Warren, Michael, 91
Washington, USA, 83
Waterford, 1, 3, 6, 8, 91
Waterford Fever Hospital, 5
Waterford House of Industry, 5
Wedgewood, 2
Weir, James, 19
Weston, Garfield, 95
Whitaker, T. K., 86
Wicklow Mountains, 73
William Street Fire Station, 24
Woods, Agnes, 68
Woods, Kathleen, 68
World War I, 39, 48, 83
World War II, 52, 55, 57, 61, 69, 79